Praise for *Walking Free*

"Micah has always been a bright light in Christian music. As a dear friend, and I'm sure so many others can say the same about him, I always find profound encouragement in his words and perspective. His newest single, "Walking Free" is a song that has such hope in it. I was overjoyed to hear it had inspired this book, filled with the same hope and wisdom to find identity in who God says you are rather than guilt and shame."

Andy Erwin, screenwriter and director of
I Can Only Imagine and *American Underdog*

"Micah is a brother that I've been able to journey with through many years. We've laughed together and even shed a few tears in our time on the road. Micah just brings an unabashed joy to others and that is the blessing of a friend he is. What most people don't know is that Micah is a pastor and although he's become an amazing singer and songwriter, his heart will always be pastoral. That is what you will read in *Walking Free*—a gift to better understand the way God pursues us and how that will inform the way we live our lives—in freedom."

Bart Millard, lead singer of MercyMe and
bestselling author of the book, *I Can Only Imagine*

"It doesn't matter if Micah is singing, speaking, or writing; he has a special way of pointing us back to the heart of Jesus. *Walking Free* is a must read for anyone looking to find a refreshing encounter with the God they serve."

Jerrad Lopes, Host of the *Dad Tired Podcast*

T0307208

WALKING FREE

WALKING FREE

TAKING SMALL STEPS TO A BIG GOD

Micah Tyler
with Robert Noland

K-LOVE
BOOKS

FRANKLIN, TENNESSEE

K-LOVE BOOKS

5700 West Oaks Blvd.
Rocklin, CA 95765

Published by K-LOVE Books, an imprint of EMF Publishing, LLC, 5700 West Oaks Blvd, Rocklin, CA 95765.

ISBN: 978-1-954201-41-5

Printed in the United States of America.

First edition: 2023
10 9 8 7 6 5 4 3 2 1

ISBN: 978-1-954201-41-5 (Hardcover)
ISBN: 978-1-954201-43-9 (E-book)
ISBN: 978-1-954201-42-2 (Audiobook)
Publisher's Cataloging-in-Publication data

Names: Tyler, Micah, author. | Noland, Robert, author.
Title: Walking free : taking small steps to a big God / by Micah Tyler; with Robert Noland.
Description: Franklin, TN: K-LOVE, 2023.
Identifiers: ISBN: 978-1-954201-41-5 (hardcover) | 978-1-954201-43-9 (ebook) | 978-1-954201-42-2 (audio)
Subjects: LCSH Christian life. | Change--Religious aspects--Christianity. | BISAC RELIGION / Christian Living / Spiritual Growth | RELIGION / Christian Living / Inspirational | SELF-HELP / Spiritual
Classification: LCC BV4501.3 .T95 2023 | DDC 248.46--dc23

Cover design by Faceout Studio, Molly von Borstel
Interior design byPerfecType, Nashville, TN

CONTENTS

Foreword by Annie F. Downs		xi
Introduction	Walking Together	1
Step 1	Baby Step to Bold Step	9
Step 2	Control to Comfort	15
Step 3	Trinket to Treasure	21
Step 4	Blindness to Belief	27
Step 5	Anxious to Adventurous	35
Step 6	Religious to Redeemed	43
Step 7	Retracing Your Steps	49
Step 8	Responsible to Reconciled	53
Step 9	Hiding to Honesty	59
Step 10	Pain to Progress	67
Step 11	Compromise to Covered	73
Step 12	Wondering to Wisdom	79
Step 13	Rebellious to Rebranded	85
Step 14	Retracing Your Steps	91
Step 15	Victim to Victor	95
Step 16	Crippled to Carried	101

CONTENTS

Step 17	Conflicted to Connected	107
Step 18	Earthly to Eternal	113
Step 19	Test to Testimony	119
Step 20	Misery to Mission	125
Step 21	Retracing Your Steps	131
Step 22	Carry to Cast	135
Step 23	Safety to Sacrifice	141
Step 24	Reckless to Relentless	147
Step 25	Useless to Useful	153
Step 26	Roaming to Rooted	159
Step 27	People-Pleaser to Peacemaker	165
Step 28	Retracing Your Steps	171
Step 29	Rules to Relationship	175
Step 30	Selfish to Submissive	181
Step 31	Superficial to Supernatural	187
Step 32	Frustration to Fulfillment	193
Step 33	Stumbling to Standing	201
Step 34	Mess to Message	207
Step 35	Retracing Your Steps	215
Step 36	Moments to Momentum	219
Step 37	Random Chance to Real Change	227
Step 38	Promise-Maker to Promise-Keeper	233
Step 39	Concealed to Consumed	241
Step 40	Merit to Mercy	247

CONTENTS

Step 41   Grief to Grace   253

Step 42   Sinner to Saint   259

WHAT'S NEXT

Retracing Your Steps   267

Walking Free—To the Finish Line   269

Walking Free Wrap-Up Review   273

Beginning a Relationship with God through
Jesus Christ   277

Thank You   281

FOREWORD
BY ANNIE F. DOWNS

I am a numbers person, which is a funny thing for an author to say. It's the way I've always been, adding up the digits on license plates, rounding to the nearest dollar, ten cents, penny, having favorite and least favorite numbers. It may be coming from a family of accountants that has the love of numbers as much a part of me as my name.

It's one of the things that makes the Bible so fun to me. It seems that over and over God uses numbers to teach us and lead us and whisper insight into our hearts.

I turned 42 this year. I'm already a big fan of 7s- born on July 7th, my jersey number was always 21 in sports. So I started talking to God pretty early about what 42 would mean to Him and mean to us. I am looking for God everywhere in my life, and that includes the amount of years on the calendar and how I spend the days that make up those years.

When I asked God what 42 meant for us, I thought of six weeks. So much can happen and so much can change in six weeks. Our family experienced great loss this summer and it feels so different six weeks after a tragedy. A relationship can be special in the first few weeks, but by six weeks, it's often either comfortable or over. A plant can grow something beautiful in six weeks, but all the leaves can go from greens to yellows to browns to covering the ground in about six weeks too. A lot can happen in 42 days.

I've been a fan of Micah Tyler's music for a long time, so when this book came across my desk, I couldn't help but smile. I find Micah to be such a wise voice, such a genuine friend to Jesus, and such an excellent storyteller. I was excited about this book before I opened it.

But then? It's split into six weeks. Into 42 days. And I knew it was a whisper from God that this was for me. And that it was no accident, for any of us, that six weeks could end up meaning a lot to us, changing us, freeing us.

Because freedom is for all of us, isn't it? No one is meant to be bound up in hurt, pain, confusion, sin, the past, the present, or fear of the future. And in 42 really small steps, Micah helps us find freedom.

I wonder how different your life could be in 42 days? If you really commit to read this book for six weeks, I wonder where you will find new freedom and new joy and new calling. I wonder if you will see subtle or substantial changes and shifts in the life you already have. I wonder what surprises God might have in store for you and I wonder what hope might be in place right when you need it.

Six weeks. 42 days. 42 opportunities to see God in new and beautiful ways through the eyes of one of our favorites, Micah Tyler. I'm excited for you as you start this journey. I'll see you on the other side of 42 days. This journey is worth it. I promise.

INTRODUCTION

Walking Together

Many years ago, as a young youth pastor, I took my students through a video Bible study from Kyle Idleman. A brief story he told affected me so much I did my own research to find out more. What I discovered forever changed the way I walk through this world.

The Great Depression was one of the toughest eras in American history. While every citizen of the country at that time was affected, the working class shouldered some of the toughest blows. With such a steep decline in production at industrial plants and mills, companies that were failing laid off their workers, causing many people to find themselves suddenly unemployed. Also, as heavy droughts killed crops, farmers and their families were left hurting and hungry all across the nation.

So, the US government decided to try to help. They developed a program to create jobs for able-bodied folks who were willing to work. People would sign up, get assigned to a project, be given the necessary tools, and then have a way to provide for themselves.

In one town, a government official hired a large crew of unemployed men for such a job. They were ecstatic, and their families wept in appreciation for this blessing at such a devastating time. The men were told to meet early one morning at the edge of a heavily wooded area, just outside of town. They were given shovels, axes, and saws to begin their assignment: build a road into the wilderness.

For these men, that road embodied their future—their freedom from despair. On their first day, they exceeded every expectation the foreman placed in front of them. The only thing louder than the sounds of trees falling to the ground was the workers' boisterous laughter and contagious excitement at once again being given the opportunity for "life, liberty, and the pursuit of happiness." The only thing stronger than the smell of fresh-cut timber hanging in the air was the dreams these men talked about as they cut a path into the future.

They asked each other hopeful questions and made positive comments like, "Where do you think this road will go?"

"Do you think it will connect to another city?"

"Maybe this will open up the opportunity for our towns to help each other."

"Maybe the city hasn't even been built yet, and one day, when travelers make their way through here, they'll be so grateful for this road!"

Morale was high and production was fierce. But after weeks of coming to work early and working late into the evening, their curiosity finally got the best of them. So, one day as they were about to start work, they decided to speak to the government official in charge of the project.

"Sir, we have to know. Please tell us where this road is headed."

His answer devastated them; it was the saddest thing these dedicated workers could ever hear. The man stated, "This road is going . . . *nowhere*. It's just a program we created for you to make money. That's it."

They had been given a job only for the sake of creating work.

With no ultimate purpose and their dreams as dead as the crops that lay in nearby fields, the men quickly lost their excitement for the project. They stopped showing up early and staying late. Productivity declined. Over the next few days, some quit coming to work altogether. Eventually, no one showed up. At the end of the road they had started to build lay a pile of abandoned saws, axes, and shovels.

In my research I found a poignant quote by preacher J. Wallace Hamilton that powerfully summed up this experience: "Roads to nowhere are hard to build."

That phrase moved something deep inside me. In my own life, I did not want to waste another moment building something without meaning. I didn't want my feet to ever carry me down a "road to nowhere." I decided to be sure I always go *somewhere*—to experience the freedom of knowing God has purpose for me on my journey. I determined to make certain my steps follow in the footprints of Jesus.

I first heard this story five years before I felt the call to serve God in Christian music. I can tell you, once He calls someone to pastor people, the ministry rarely changes, but the location can. Now, it's not only my family and the people I serve in my local body, but everyone I meet out on the road and the people who listen to my music. But no matter the size of the crowd in an arena or church, or even if I'm having a heart-to-heart with one person, I know my steps are purposefully headed *somewhere* God wants me to be.

One thing I've discovered since becoming a Christian artist and songwriter—your life will soon be challenged on *any* song you write and release that comes from the truth of God's Word. Take "Walking Free," for example, the inspiration for the title and theme of this book. My younger brother, Daniel, has battled cancer twice. He was first diagnosed in 2017 and eventually beat it. Then in 2020, we were told the disease had returned. He had surgery to remove the tumor, and, thank God, they got it. His scans came back clean, and Daniel was able to "ring the bell" for the second time.

The truth is that when a crisis such as life-threatening cancer occurs, we can feel like our spiritual freedom is suddenly gone and our purpose to keep building roads is challenged. We can even feel robbed and violated. Fear, anxiety, and despair can begin to rule our hearts. As a Christ-follower, we know that circumstances in this life never dictate His power to overcome *anything*. But that doesn't automatically negate the deep internal struggle we face when life comes crashing down. The question is, Will we walk in His freedom or stand frozen in fear? Surrendering the fight to Jesus can feel difficult to do but is always a game-changer.

In mid-2022, just as I began writing this book, my brother found out his cancer was back for a third time. The report indicated the presence of multiple tumors. As soon as I got home from my tour, I began driving him back and forth to treatments in Houston. Each time, the risks and the stakes get higher because the chemo has already devastated his body. But my brother, a youth pastor like I was, is so determined in his life and committed to his faith that he will endure treatment one day and be right back with the students in his ministry the next. He refuses to let cancer keep him from the purpose God has given him. I'm here to tell you that Daniel is a living, breathing testimony to walking free with Christ *through* the circumstances. Not around, not over or under, but through.

Daniel also proves that being committed to Jesus never comes with a guarantee that life will be easy and trouble-free. But the promise Christ made was to remain with us in any hardship. Sometimes He does rescue us, and sometimes the healing comes. Other times, He carries us into the fire. In those circumstances, when we have every reason to fall down and obey fear's authority, we must rely instead on God's perfect love, the greatest Force in this life. No matter the road, He calls us to build it so that we may walk in the freedom only He can give, inviting others to walk with us.

With Daniel's circumstances, I have had to constantly remind myself that we have full access to God's armor. In Ephesians 6, when Paul teaches us to put on all the pieces for battle, he never tells us when it's safe to take it off. So, that must mean we leave it on throughout life until we get to the gates of Heaven. There and only there, we will no longer need the protection. God promises all the suffering, pain, disease, tears, and ravages of this world will be gone forever. But until then, His armor is part of His provision to walk in freedom.

The steps within these pages are simply the ways in which I point my *own* heart back toward God's truth on the hard days while storing it up on the good days. My hope and prayer for you is to share that experience with me as we walk

together. You may be going through something really difficult right now and the *last* thing you feel is freedom. You feel
like you're building a road to nowhere, and like those men,
you may want to throw down your tools and walk away. *Trust
me, I get it.* But, speaking from firsthand experience, I want to
encourage you that walking in the freedom of Christ is available to you in and through His grace and mercy. If it's true for
me, it's true for you. That's the way the gospel works. That's
why the gospel works.

I'm inviting you to join me on a forty-five-day journey
as we take small steps away from the things of this world and
all the empty promises it offers and walk toward the good
things of God and the knowledge of knowing Jesus more
deeply and meaningfully. Understand, though, this book is
not about hoping that if we can get forty-five things right,
we can become free. The Christian life is not a checklist,
but, rather, a relationship with the Author of freedom. The
moment that begins and we are forgiven of our sins, we
are fully, completely acquitted, set free from the penalty of
sin and death. Believing that one day we can become good
enough or someday arrive at perfection is a religious lie. Jesus
offers us liberty *in spite* of all the trappings of sin. He wants
to lovingly teach us how to experience and enjoy the fruit of
our freedom in Christ.

That's why I want to be really clear about one thing: I
am not on the other end of the road pointing back at you,
calling out the how-to instructions toward freedom. *Not at
all.* We'll take these steps *together*, working toward trusting the Lord, because we don't follow each other, we follow
Him. As we walk this journey, we want to celebrate God's
love for us, discovering the heights that His freedom brings

into our lives. Our prayer will be the same one my family has been offering up for the past several years: "Lord, help us to trust you more today than yesterday." We'll take one step at a time, constantly reminding each other of our Father's kindness and goodness.

So, let's do it. Let's pick up the tools that God has equipped us with and head into the wilderness. Together, we can build roads of purpose so we can walk in His freedom. Some steps will be beautiful and some will be difficult, but this road will lead somewhere amazing. One step at a time!

As we get started, consider establishing a goal with a purpose. Take a few minutes to prayerfully answer these questions in the space provided.

Next-Step Questions

What kind of road are you building in your life right now? Are you headed toward freedom or away from it?

_____

_____

What does freedom look like for you? Do your best to describe it.

_____

_____

What do you most want God to accomplish in you by the end of these forty-five steps?

_____

_____

For the Lord is the *SPIRIT*, and wherever the Spirit of the Lord is, there is freedom.

—2 Corinthians 3:17

STEP

01

Baby Step to Bold Step

I remember with each one of my three children the moment they committed to taking their first steps. You could see that gleam in their eyes just before they lifted a tiny foot and gave it a shot. Whether each child was able to take a few steps or fell right away, it was their one and only *first* baby step. But, that first step out was also a bold step. Why? Because it's the moment they finally made the decision to create their own movement. Crawling was no longer enough. Scooting didn't cut it anymore. Watching everyone else get from point A to point B was over. Independence was waiting on the other side of that decision to step out.

Just because we're adults doesn't mean taking first steps gets any easier. In fact, so often, it's harder. Stepping out has risks and consequences. When we feel like it's time for a new journey or a fresh start, the old saying applies at any age or stage of life: "The hardest step is always the first one."

For some, it feels like a huge, scary leap off the edge of a cliff. Perhaps to end something, like deciding to call the addiction recovery center for help. Or to start something, like putting notice in at a job to launch out into a new venture. For others, it's a tiny step, like finally choosing the salad over the cheeseburger or whispering a prayer for the first time in a very long time. The circumstances around our challenges shape our perception of what it actually takes to bring about real change.

But, when we talk about walking free, especially in a spiritual sense, what does that really mean? Let's look at Jesus's words in John 8:31–36.

> Jesus said to the people who believed in him, "You are truly my disciples if you remain faithful to my teachings. And you will know the truth, and the truth will set you free."
>
> "But we are descendants of Abraham," they said. "We have never been slaves to anyone. What do you mean, 'You will be set free'?"
>
> Jesus replied, "I tell you the truth, everyone who sins is a slave of sin. A slave is not a permanent member of the family, but a son is part of the family forever. So if the Son sets you free, you are truly free."

The people listening to Jesus were obviously confused. They thought He meant physical freedom, when he was talking about being set free from slavery to sin. He was declaring Himself as the Messiah, the Savior, but they struggled to understand their need for Him—just like people have in every generation, especially today. At any particular time, whether we are up on top of the mountain or deep in the darkness of the valley, we all have sin that is constantly trying to enslave us. For the nonbeliever, that slavery is a reality, and the lure to fall even deeper is always there. For the believer, freedom has come, but sin still constantly calls out to return to its grasp. Spiritual slavery is not an event but a life condition. That's why sin is never satisfied with a single act and always seeks recognition, attention, repetition, and addiction.

But, as sinners, we also have an open invitation from a Savior. Someone who calls us to Him, regardless of how far we have fallen or how bulletproof we might feel. Someone who calls us to go further and higher than we have ever gone before and get closer to Him than we ever imagined possible. Like Jesus said, "If *I* set you free, you are truly free."

So, the first step to walking in freedom is to accept and receive the invitation of Jesus. To personally receive the truth of the gospel. Invite Him to change everything, to make all things new.

> But God showed his great love for us by sending Christ to die for us while we were still sinners. And since we have been made right in God's sight by the blood of Christ, he will certainly save us from God's condemnation. (Romans 5:8–9)

No matter what you've gone through, or what may have been done to you, whatever relationships you've had or never had, the hurts you've suffered or the number of people you've hurt, Christ's death and resurrection offers true freedom from the past. As we just read, through "his great love . . . we have been made right" and are certainly saved from condemnation.

Not only that, but in a relationship with Jesus, He leads our steps by determining both *priority* and *purpose*. In Him, that will never be about how big the step is or how far down the road we get but about being intentional. Far too many people stay stuck because they believe their first step has to be a huge leap. That's simply not true. With God, whether an inch or a mile, it's the forward progress that counts. Whether crawling or running, stay focused on Christ. In everything we do, the opportunity to take not only the first step but the *next* step will bring us closer to Him.

Regardless of our spiritual state, we all know this life is full of personal battles. Our calling is to remember that in Christ we can still move forward, even when the way is difficult or when our trust falters. We must put our focus on Him rather than whatever stands in our way. It's sometimes easier said than done, especially when the trials of this world push in. But as my pastor once said, "I'm so tired of having more faith in the arrows that are being fired at me than the shield that God has given to protect me. I don't want to have more faith in the weapons formed *against me* than I do in the protection He has provided *for me*. While all I have is His shield, His shield is *all* I need."

> But in that coming day
> > no weapon turned against you will succeed.
> You will silence every voice
> > raised up to accuse you.
> These benefits are enjoyed by the servants of the
> Lord;
> > their vindication will come from me.
> > I, the Lord, have spoken! (Isaiah 54:17)

When we trust in the things of this world more than we exercise the faith that God has already instilled in our hearts, we can become stagnant and frozen, unable to move forward.

But the truth is that Jesus will fight for us, He will always go before us, and He has set us free, regardless of how we may feel. He has already provided all we need through His death on the cross and His resurrection from the dead. The work of salvation has been done. It *is* finished! Our calling is simply to take each baby step of faith—every bold step in Him—to walk in His freedom.

If you have never begun a relationship with God through Jesus Christ, turn to page 279. If you aren't certain where you stand in your relationship with Him, you can go to that page as well. A number and link are available there to contact a pastor for help.

Next-Step Questions

Describe your moment of surrender to Jesus and your acceptance of the gospel for the first time.

_____

_____

A bold step of faith is to understand that Jesus has already accomplished all you need for life and salvation. Where do you stand today in accepting that truth?

_____

_____

Whether a baby step or a bold step, what step of faith are you going to take today?

_____

_____

Because **WALKING** in
faith is never one-size-fits-all,
every step toward Jesus
is *BOLD*.

Control to Comfort

Everything in life begins with a need—real or perceived. I'm hungry. I'm cold. I'm angry. I'm bored. Being self-centered by nature, we desperately want two things 24-7: comfort and control. Because we feel the most comforted when we are in control, we want to control life to stay comfortable. Losing control is uncomfortable.

Therefore, whenever we express how we feel, there is usually a need attached. The question is whether each need is a necessity or a want. There are a lot of things in this life that we don't need yet we want. We can prioritize luxuries right next to necessities. We tend to mix those up a lot. Any time we believe the luxuries in our lives don't meet our needs, we're in trouble.

But, we have to understand that spiritual freedom is not a luxury. Salvation is not a luxury. The gospel is not a luxury. They are all a necessity. Why? Because of our need.

We are lost. We are separated from God with no way to save ourselves. Romans 3:23 states that we have all fallen short of His glory. Even the best among us cannot make it to Him. For everyone, sin—disobedience to God—is all we can produce. And the result is death. This is not something we can control.

But Jesus, the One who did not know sin yet became sin, through His kindness made the choice to offer us His righteousness. He has invited us to His table, where not only our needs will be met, but we will be loved. We can exchange our control for His comfort.

> For the sin of this one man, Adam, caused death to rule over many. But even greater is God's wonderful grace and his gift of righteousness, for all who receive it will live in triumph over sin and death through this one man, Jesus Christ. (Romans 5:17)

His promise offers not just an assurance to escape hell at death, but to have abundant life here and eternal life one day. We are given His peace and grace, along with access to all His character and qualities. The finest luxuries this world has to offer cannot compare to Him meeting the needs of our souls.

I once heard a story about a farmer who had a very happy flock of sheep, all content in his pasture. One day, another farmer bought the neighboring property and put up a fence on the boundary line. He soon moved in his own flock of sheep. As the original sheep began to watch, they realized the new farmer was giving out better food and offering more attention to his sheep than they had ever received from their owner.

As all the original sheep began to gather at the fence line, wishing for what they saw, the new farmer came over, opened a small hole at the bottom of the fence, and said, "You all are more than welcome to come over to my pasture. You've seen how I treat my sheep."

A few of the sheep immediately moved away from the man, retreating deeper into their own pasture, uncertain of this new voice and presence. Others stayed right up at the fence to keep watching, thinking about going through. But some decided they wanted to take the man up on his offer for better pasture right then, so they crawled through the hole and joined his flock.

The next morning, the original sheep who had remained in their field heard a horrible sound—the bleating and crying of *all* the sheep in the new farmer's pasture, including their friends. As they watched in horror, they realized every sheep that had gone over to the other side of the fence had been lured to the slaughter. The difference between life and death, between comfort and control, was just one step to the other side of that fence.

That's exactly what the enemy does in tempting us to go past God's boundaries—and why another word for "sin" is *trespass*. We have to remind ourselves that sin will *never* look out for our good. Sin gives us the illusion of control. It exists only to kill, steal, and destroy our lives through selfishness, self-absorption, and self-destruction.

The unsolvable problem for us was that sin had enslaved us. God's permanent solution is to offer us His freedom. Through the Lord's kindness, not His wrath, the opportunity to repent—to turn and walk the opposite way from sin—is available. Because Jesus came for us and to us in His mercy.

Don't you see how wonderfully kind, tolerant, and patient God is with you? Does this mean nothing to you? Can't you see that his kindness is intended to turn you from your sin? (Romans 2:4)

We will never be good enough on our own merit. We can't pray hard enough or sacrifice enough. This is why His goodness, faithfulness, and mercy are offered to us. Christianity is the only belief system in which God does not sit on a throne and say, "Work hard enough and you might get to me." Instead, He left His throne and met us right where we are in the midst of our sin. Instead, He says, "I'll bring goodness to you and walk alongside you through any difficulty." He already knows what we're going through. He already knows how hard these steps are to take. He already knows the things we're carrying and the weight we have on us right now. As we take steps of faith, we have the ability at any point to reach out to Him, and say, "Lord, I need help laying these things down and trusting your peace over my fear."

Jesus, having gone before us, has offered us the victory that He won when He stepped out from Heaven and laid down his life. He is continually calling to us, "Come and follow me." Following in the steps He's already taken, we can walk free from our own need to control what we cannot control anyway. We can walk forward in faith and trust Him to comfort us through anything we may face.

Connecting to the story I shared about the sheep, in John 10, Jesus likened Himself to a shepherd. Pay close attention to His promises here.

"I tell you the truth, anyone who sneaks over the wall of a sheepfold, rather than going through the gate, must surely be a thief and a robber! But the one who enters through the gate is the shepherd of the sheep. The gatekeeper opens the gate for him, and the sheep recognize his voice and come to him. He calls his own sheep by name and leads them out. After he has gathered his own flock, he walks ahead of them, and they follow him because they know his voice. They won't follow a stranger; they will run from him because they don't know his voice. . . .

"I tell you the truth, I am the gate for the sheep. . . . Those who come in through me will be saved. They will come and go freely and will find good pastures. The thief's purpose is to steal and kill and destroy. My purpose is to give them a rich and satisfying life. . . .

"The good shepherd sacrifices his life for the sheep. . . . I am the good shepherd; I know my own sheep, and they know me, just as my Father knows me and I know the Father. So I sacrifice my life for the sheep. . . . They will listen to my voice, and there will be one flock with one shepherd." (John 10:1–5, 7, 9–11, 14–16)

As one final reminder, if you have never begun a relationship with God through Jesus Christ, turn to page 279. If you aren't certain where you stand in your relationship with Him, you can go to that page as well. A number and link are available there to contact a pastor for help.

Next-Step Questions

On a scale from one to ten, how much do you work to control your world? Explain your score.

_____

_____

How can learning to trust Jesus with your life allow you to let go of control and trust in His comfort as your Shepherd?

_____

_____

Moving from your control to His comfort, what is your one step of faith to take today?

_____

_____

Each step away from the
need to *CONTROL*
allows us to step into the
COMFORT of Christ.

Trinket to Treasure

In the book of Exodus, when Pharaoh finally relented and told Moses to take the Israelites and leave, an interesting passage follows:

> And the people of Israel did as Moses had instructed; they asked the Egyptians for clothing and articles of silver and gold. The LORD caused the Egyptians to look favorably on the Israelites, and they gave the Israelites whatever they asked for. So they stripped the Egyptians of their wealth! (Exodus 12:35–36)

One of the most valuable and cherished things the Egyptians handed over would have been their gold jewelry. Now, fast-forward to Exodus 32:1–4:

> When the people saw how long it was taking Moses to come back down the mountain, they gathered around Aaron. "Come on," they said, "make us some

gods who can lead us. We don't know what happened to this fellow Moses, who brought us here from the land of Egypt."

So Aaron said, "Take the gold rings from the ears of your wives and sons and daughters, and bring them to me."

All the people took the gold rings from their ears and brought them to Aaron. Then Aaron took the gold, melted it down, and molded it into the shape of a calf. When the people saw it, they exclaimed, "O Israel, these are the gods who brought you out of the land of Egypt!"

God allowed the Israelites to have the jewelry for two likely reasons. One was simply a blessing to enjoy after coming out of literal captivity. Anything of value and beauty would have never been allowed when they were slaves. The jewelry became symbols of a new day, a reflection of being God's chosen and freed people. The second reason was practical: His provision. They could always sell the pieces to provide for their families for many years to come.

By ignoring God's provision in so many ways, in their moment of weakness and vulnerability, sin called out to take them captive in a different way. Not in the physical this time, but the spiritual. The treasures they were given to walk into a brand-new life quickly became something to misuse, to waste, and, oddly, to worship. They traded what God had provided to enslave themselves again, this time to an idol. Bottom line—they handed over their freedom with one bad decision.

While it can be really hard for us to understand why they would create a golden idol and then announce that this thing they just made with their own hands was what gave them their freedom from Egypt, we sometimes commit the very same sin. We sometimes take a gift from God and waste it—and even worship it instead of Him. Trade in His treasure for the world's trinkets.

There is no question that God opened the door for me to work and serve in Christian music. But, what if one day I am presented with a gold record? Could I be tempted to become impressed with myself and my music career? Certainly. Could I hang it up in my living room and begin to worship the created rather than the Creator? Of course. In fact, I wouldn't have to melt down a gold record to choose to worship it. Could I start to trust in my talent instead of Him? Sure. The attitude of my heart would create the same outcome as the Israelites with their golden calf.

But then what if my next album isn't as successful? If I have put my faith in my own ability, fear will start to reign because I have traded the treasure of God for a trinket, given to me by the world. Even a career singing about Jesus can be turned from freedom back to slavery. We can create an idol from most anything. That's what sin wants to do.

This side of Heaven, Satan's battle will never stop as he tries to get us to trade treasure for trinkets. In Luke 4, Jesus was in the wilderness alone, fasting. Satan began to use the same old tactic he used on Adam and Eve. He altered the "Did God really say . . . ?" question from the garden into "If you are the Son of God . . ." challenge in the desert. He tried to get Jesus to end His spiritual fast by turning stones to bread. To take His glory now by bowing down to worship Satan. To jump off the pinnacle to prove that God would protect Him. The goal was to do anything to keep Jesus from the cross, from redeeming God's creation.

With each try, even though Jesus was physically, emotionally, and mentally weakened by hunger, thirst, and exhaustion, He called on His faith by quoting passages from the Torah to the enemy. And finally, after three strikes and a strong rebuke, the devil left. Jesus didn't trade His treasure for the trinkets dangled before Him. His faith won out. His faith made Him strong in weakness and brought glory to God.

The Israelites showed us the consequences of choosing sin, while Jesus gave us proof of the best choice, the right decision. Satan will always wave his trinkets in front of us when we are vulnerable and exposed. In those moments, we must remind ourselves to take our next step toward Jesus. In fact, to run to Him. There, we will find strength, security, and safety. He alone is the Treasure in our lives.

Next-Step Questions

Has there been a time in your life when fear got the best of you and you found something else to replace God? Explain.

_____

_____

Describe a time when you chose the treasure by expressing your faith in Christ in the midst of a tough situation.

_____

_____

Setting aside trinkets to pursue the treasure of God, what step of faith can you take today?

_____

_____

When trinkets are dangled before you, keep your eyes on the *TREASURE*.

STEP

04

Blindness to Belief

One thing we can quickly learn about being in a relationship with God is that He rarely takes away all our pain in a day, in a week, or even in the course of going through a book like this. Does He sometimes do that? Of course, depending on the person and his or her circumstances. Can He heal anything, anytime? Yes, because He's God. As Jesus stated in Mark 9:23, "Anything is possible if a person believes." But, learning to walk in freedom is a day-by-day lifelong process.

Take Paul, for instance. In 2 Corinthians 5:7, he stated that we "walk by faith, not by sight" (ESV). We have to remember that after he was confronted by Jesus on the road to Damascus, Paul was blind for a time. When his spiritual eyes were opened forever, his physical eyes were temporarily closed. He was suddenly thrown into a world of darkness and had to rely totally on this new faith that had interrupted his life. He had to listen to and obey Jesus because he could not see and had nowhere else to turn.

Before we begin to walk by faith, we are not blind to *sight* but, rather, blind to *belief*. Sighted people can look ahead in the physical sense but not in the spiritual. We can't see the future, so we have to *believe* before we can *see* in faith.

As we begin to walk on a deeper level in our relationship with Christ, one of the first things we need to see is that we will have to carry our pain into the journey. Just like Paul's blindness, our struggles will be with us as we take our next steps. Sometimes, they might even get worse before they get better. Often, God will call us to deal with something difficult when we have ignored it for a long time. For this reason, when we walk by faith, we can no longer measure or compare ourselves to what anybody else around us is doing. We must trust that God will be with us, He will sustain us, He will watch over us, He will fill us, and He will surround us with the strength we need in each moment to help us keep taking steps.

Just before Jesus made His triumphal entry into Jerusalem, He had an encounter with a very loud blind man.

> Then they reached Jericho, and as Jesus and his disciples left town, a large crowd followed him. A blind beggar named Bartimaeus (son of Timaeus) was sitting beside the road. When Bartimaeus heard that Jesus of Nazareth was nearby, he began to shout, "Jesus, Son of David, have mercy on me!"
>
> "Be quiet!" many of the people yelled at him.
>
> But he only shouted louder, "Son of David, have mercy on me!"

When Jesus heard him, he stopped and said, "Tell him to come here."

So they called the blind man. "Cheer up," they said. "Come on, he's calling you!" Bartimaeus threw aside his coat, jumped up, and came to Jesus.

"What do you want me to do for you?" Jesus asked.

"My Rabbi," the blind man said, "I want to see!"

And Jesus said to him, "Go, for your faith has healed you." Instantly the man could see, and he followed Jesus down the road. (Mark 10:46–52)

Let's work through a few truths to better understand this passage, starting with the context. In that day, if someone had a disability that did not allow him or her to work, begging for money was common. Folks with various ailments and issues would line the side of the road. As people came into the city, many would throw coins toward them. Some were probably compassionate and intentional, maybe giving to a certain person every time. Others may have made it more of a cruel sport, watching them clamor for a coin thrown close by.

Now that we understand the basics, let's look further:

- In that time, blindness was considered a curse from God. An immediate cultural and spiritual stigma came with not having sight. The general belief was that the person or the person's family had sinned in some horrible way to receive God's permanent judgment. The discrimination would have been a constant source of shame for a blind person, much like leprosy and other suffering was also viewed.

- Beggars had a cloak that they would lay out in front of them as they sat down for the day. Because the person was very poor, the cloak would have been one of their only possessions, likely their most valued. But that also meant the cloak defined their disability, their limitation, their poverty, their isolation from society.
- The cloak also acted as a sort of boundary line for any coins that were tossed their way. If a coin landed on the person's cloak, it was theirs. In the music world, busking is when a singer or musician plays on the street for money. For guitar players, the open guitar case is typically where people put bills or coins as a tip. While a very different concept than the cloak, the purpose is the same. Whether a ten-dollar bill thrown into a guitar case or a coin thrown onto the cloak, it offers a marked territory for what people give.

Based on what we know historically about that era, Bartimaeus was most likely alone. No wife. No family of his own. He would wake up every day and wait for someone to come pick him up or lead him back to the street, where he would sit on the side of the road and beg all day long, relying on the compassion or pity of passersby. Judging by the people's reactions to him, Bartimaeus was a regular on that street. He was sitting there on the edge of his cloak, just like any typical day, hoping to get enough coins tossed his way to be able to eat.

But, here's another example of how, when Jesus showed up, everything changed. Bartimaeus had evidently heard about Christ and then found out He was walking within ear-shot. So, he started shouting, "Son of David, have mercy on me!" He was literally crying out to get Jesus's attention, try-ing to be heard above the crowd. The people quickly became annoyed and told Bartimaeus to shut up. But he'd seen his chance, and he was going to take it.

Throughout the Gospels, it's always fascinating to see what Jesus did when He decided to help someone. When He heard Bartimaeus, an obvious blind man, did He walk over to him and kneel down? *No.* He said, "Tell him to come here." Jesus had the guy get up and walk to Him, literally by faith and not by sight. We don't know whether it was a few feet or half a block.

So, what was Bartimaeus's response? *Watch this.* He threw aside his cloak, jumped up, and came to Christ. The cloak, his prized possession, was no longer the focus. It was Jesus.

The next interesting thing that Christ did was ask Bartimaeus, "What do you want me to do for you?" Jesus made the blind man tell Him what he wanted. He was saying not to make assumptions. Speak it in faith. Be specific about your need. In that moment, Bartimaeus's identification of the Lord changed from "Son of David," a recognition of his Jewish heri-tage, to "my Rabbi," my spiritual leader, my pastor, if you will.

Bartimaeus answered, "I want to see." In that moment, Jesus told him that his faith gave him sight.

And then in the final verse, where were Bartimaeus's next steps? Following Jesus. Now, by faith *and* sight!

Do you think Bartimaeus ever went back and got his cloak? We don't know, but why *would* he? Why *should* he? Do you think the next day, he went back to the side of the street to beg? We don't know, but why *would* he? Why *should* he?

As we talked about earlier, sometimes Jesus chooses *not* to take away whatever our "blindness" may be. But should that cause us to *not* step out in faith toward Him? Do we make it about the healing or about Him? That's exactly why we call it faith. Belief. Whether Jesus chooses to fix the problem today or not, we need to trust Him by taking the next step anyway.

Remember, Bartimaeus didn't know if Jesus was going to help him. The first evidence of the change in him was leaving behind his cloak *before* he was healed. He made a fool of himself in front of the crowd, then got up and walked in blindness to Jesus. But, he was bold enough to say, "I want to be healed." Deciding to get up and take those steps, however many there were, changed his life forever. He went from blindness to belief.

Next-Step Questions

What is your "blindness" (anything that keeps you from seeing God's plan) and what would be your "cloak" (the identity you've placed on yourself from your past)?

_____

_____

How might focusing on belief in Jesus, rather than the "blindness" or the "cloak," change your life right now?

_____

_____

What is your one step of faith to take today in moving from blindness to belief?

_____

_____

Be **SPECIFIC** in
your prayers
so you can be
STRATEGIC
in your steps.

Anxious to Adventurous

The story of Peter stepping out of the boat to walk on the water toward Jesus is one of the most well known in the gospels. Ironically, Peter gets a bad rap for his actions. How many thousands, maybe millions, of sermons have included something like, "But poor, poor Peter just didn't have enough faith to get to Jesus and the Lord had to save him from drowning when he sank"?

Are you kidding me? Really? The guy who crawled out of the boat and tried to head toward Jesus . . . on . . . the . . . water . . . in . . . the . . . storm . . . is the one who will be forever criticized for his "lack of faith"? That hardly seems fair, does it? After all, who still holds the record in the history of the world for being second in water walking? Who has the silver medal in most steps taken on water? The guy who catches all the flack in this story—Peter. (And allow me to add, the rest of us are tied for last place.)

When Peter saw Jesus, even with the wind and the waves threatening, he went right out into the water. What did the other disciples do? They sat in the boat, watching the whole thing. Probably thinking something like, *Peter gon' die.* But, no matter how well you think you know the story, in today's step, try looking at it with different eyes and hearing with different ears.

Meanwhile, the disciples were in trouble far away from land, for a strong wind had risen, and they were fighting heavy waves. About three o'clock in the morning Jesus came toward them, walking on the water. When the disciples saw him walking on the water, they were terrified. In their fear, they cried out, "It's a ghost!"

But Jesus spoke to them at once. "Don't be afraid," he said. "Take courage. I am here!" Then Peter called to him, "Lord, if it's really you, tell me to come to you, walking on the water." "Yes, come," Jesus said. So Peter went over the side of the boat and walked on the water toward Jesus. But when he saw the strong wind and the waves, he was terrified and began to sink. "Save me, Lord!" he shouted.

Jesus immediately reached out and grabbed him. "You have so little faith," Jesus said. "Why did you doubt me?" When they climbed back into the boat, the wind stopped. Then the disciples worshiped him. "You really are the Son of God!" they exclaimed. (Matthew 14:24–33)

Look again at verse 29: "So Peter went over the side of the boat and walked on the water toward Jesus." How many steps was that? Three or thirty? We don't know. We aren't told. But does it really matter? The facts are clear. For some distance, he walked on water, just like Jesus was doing. Despite Peter's inhibition and fear, he was the only disciple to step out. Even though he was fully aware that he was walking *on* something incredibly unsafe, Peter knew he was walking *toward* the greatest safety he would ever find—Jesus. Something that looked *insecure* would become his greatest *security*.

Likely, the reason why so many pastors, priests, and Sunday school teachers have criticized Peter is because of what Jesus told him: "You have so little faith. Why did you doubt me?" But, consider this: if the guy who got out and tried to walk on the water but sank is told, "You have so little faith," what could be said about the guys curled up in the fetal position in the boat? They didn't express *any* faith. They didn't doubt, because they never even believed! Yet after Jesus helped Peter back into the boat, *all* the disciples worshiped and declared Christ as the Son of God.

Who in this story would have experienced the most anxiousness? Well, while they were all afraid of the wind, the waves, and the potential of drowning in the storm, Peter's anxiety was at an eleven when he began to sink into the water. But who then experienced one of the greatest adventures in human history? Yep, same guy.

Comedian Brian Regan has done a bit for years in which he talks about the twelve astronauts who walked on the moon. Regan says that in any room at any party, no matter what anyone brags about doing to impress the group, all one of those guys has to do is wait until the braggart is done and then simply say, "I walked on the moon." Because no one can top that.

Of the twelve men who followed Jesus, only one could say he walked on the water with Him. I wonder if, when Peter and John were preaching to thousands after Jesus had ascended into Heaven, some kid ever walked up afterward and asked, "So, what was it like when you walked on the water? And in a storm even?" I wonder if Peter smiled and answered, "Well, kid, it was one incredible adventure."

What about you? Right now, is Jesus challenging you in some area of your life, and you're thinking, *This doesn't feel safe at all, but maybe I'm supposed to step out and do this thing?* Could your maxed-out anxiety turn into the most incredible adventure you've ever experienced?

I know how that feels. Over the past several years, I have talked to a lot of young musicians who heard my story about how our family sold over half of what we owned and bought a little mobile home, and I left my secure church position in Buna, Texas. There was no record deal or tour dates, just a call to be faithful. To make ends meet, I took on odd jobs like making deliveries, substitute teaching, and mowing lawns. The goal was having the freedom to play wherever and for whomever God called me.

I always have to stress that *He* called *us* to that radical obedience. He helped us walk every step of the way. Unfortunately, when it comes to music, so many people want so desperately to be famous that they make choices and sacrifices like ours that would never work. What might feel like an adventure at first can end up creating terrible anxiety, especially if God is not in it. (Believe me—there's plenty of anxiety even when you know you are in His will.) But, I didn't—and don't—want to be famous. I just want to be faithful. To love Jesus the best I can.

That is what we are *all* called to do. But how we each accomplish that will be very different. Whatever God leads you to do might not be the same thing as me. Each person's calling will look totally different, and everyone's adventure with Him will be as customized as the uniqueness of the circumstances. The goal, however, is the same: for you and me to go from the boat to the water with Jesus, where the true adventure of life will always be. If you ask anyone who has fully surrendered their life to Christ if there are dull and mundane days, the answer is going to be, "Of course." But is life ever boring? Never.

> I came so they can have real and eternal life, more and better life than they ever dreamed of. (John 10:10 MSG)

In the end, it's not about boring or exciting but only about following Christ. I once heard a missionary tell the story of being a teacher in a country that was hostile to Christianity. On many days he and his family had to hide away, rationing their food and water, trying to not be found. They would have to wait for the all-clear from the locals that it was safe to come out and resume their work. These events were very scary to their family. But, here's a paraphrase of how he ended his testimony:

> You're probably thinking something, so let me go ahead and answer the question. As I speak in churches across the United States, people ask me, "Hey man, why would you do that to your family? Don't you believe that their safety is more important than any job you could take? Why would you take

that risk? Can't you get a job as a teacher here in the States where your kids don't have to hide in a closet for days?" This is my honest answer: The safest place for my family is always in the will of God. . . . There's no place safer for us. . . . I could be a teacher at a school right down the road from here, and it could be the most dangerous place if it's not what God wants me to be doing.

The point is, as Christ-followers, we must decide that words and concepts like *safety*, *security*, and *risk* are going to have to be redefined in the realm of faith. But then, so will words like *exciting*, *fulfilling*, *satisfying*, and *adventurous*. The more steps we take in faith, the more that His paradigm will be created in our lives. Yes, we live in this world, but we also live inside Christ—in His economy, protection, provision, mission, and calling.

Yesterday, we saw how Jesus called Bartimaeus to come to Him. Today, we see how He responded to Peter's request, "Lord, if it's really you, tell me to come to you, walking on the water."

Jesus answered, "Yes, come." Did He make the storm weaker? No. Did He make the water any less dangerous? No. Did He make water-walking easy? No, obviously not. But was Peter ever in any real danger? No. He wasn't, because of just one thing—the presence of Jesus. As you walk from anxiety into adventure with Christ, you will discover the same to be true for you.

Next-Step Questions

What is creating the most anxiety in your life right now? Explain.

_____

_____

Is God calling you to step out and take an adventure, but you're anxious about safety and security? Write out your thoughts.

_____

_____

Focusing on the adventure of walking with Jesus, what is your one step of faith to take today?

_____

_____

The most *SECURE*
place in life
may not always be the
SAFEST.

STEP

06

———————

Religious to Redeemed

As we talked about yesterday, so much of walking through this life with Jesus is about constantly stepping from the known to the unknown. Our sin causes us to try to stay in the comfort zone, on the safe path. That's why Jesus said the way to Him "is very narrow and the road is difficult, and only a few ever find it" (Matthew 7:14). It's not that it's hard to locate His way, but once you do, it's not an *easy* road to walk.

Religion has long been defined as people trying to reach up to God on their own, through their own terms. We know this to be true from the countless belief systems that have been created throughout history. But God's redemption was made available to us when He came down to us in Jesus. He made the way when there was no way. We had nothing to do with it.

Today, our step is about leaving behind the religious baggage of trying to win God's approval and accepting that Jesus has redeemed us—paid our debt of disobedience in full—along with the ransom our sin created. He alone gives us freedom. He ended our captivity from the eternal consequences of the choice that began in the Garden. That is redemption.

It's ironic and interesting that Jesus's constant battle, between the devil's temptations in the desert and His arrest that led to the cross, was with the religious leaders of the day—the ones who should have been helping God's people on the path to redemption. When Jesus wanted to show the people how *not* to live out their faith, He often used them as examples.

> Then Jesus told this story to some who had great confidence in their own righteousness and scorned everyone else: "Two men went to the Temple to pray. One was a Pharisee, and the other was a despised tax collector. The Pharisee stood by himself and prayed this prayer: 'I thank you, God, that I am not like other people—cheaters, sinners, adulterers. I'm certainly not like that tax collector! I fast twice a week, and I give you a tenth of my income.'
>
> "But the tax collector stood at a distance and dared not even lift his eyes to heaven as he prayed. Instead, he beat his chest in sorrow, saying, 'O God, be merciful to me, for I am a sinner.' I tell you, this sinner, not the Pharisee, returned home justified before God. For those who exalt themselves will be humbled, and those who humble themselves will be exalted." (Luke 18:9–14)

Now, understand that back then, people had been conditioned to honor the Pharisees and hate the tax collectors.

That was the cultural norm of the day. So, whether this was an actual situation that Jesus knew about or was completely hypothetical, for Him to make the Pharisee look bad and the tax collector look good, those were fighting words. This was a big, bold statement and comparison. Let's look at what He stated.

The Pharisee's prayer
- communicated publicly for everyone to hear,
- was condescending toward those "other people,"
- confessed "other people's" sins, not his own,
- compared himself to a hated position for his own glory, and
- was conceited about his behavior and "sacrifice."

The tax collector's prayer
- communicated privately in humility,
- condemned himself,
- confessed his own sin,
- compared himself to God's law, and
- conceded his desperation before God.

The biggest difference between the prayers of these two men was the attitude of their hearts. The Pharisee focused totally on his external behavior, as in, "Look at what I haven't done that's bad and then look at all I have done that's good." That is religion. Focus on *do*. The tax collector zeroed in on the state of his heart, as in, "God, I don't even deserve to look Your way, but please give me Your mercy for my wrongs." That is redemption. Focus on *be*.

One of the most destructive things we can do is compare ourselves to other people. This can happen in two ways. The first is what the Pharisee did. He exalted himself by claiming how much better he was than someone else. (This lies at the root of issues such as racism, classism, status, and so on.) He became his own standard, which never works. The second is very popular in our culture today: comparing ourselves to people we believe are better than us or have something better than us, whether appearance, talent, or a possession. The other person becomes the standard, which also never works. (Without this one, social media probably wouldn't have caught on.)

Either way, when we start comparing ourselves to others, we usually begin making excuses for our own behavior. The result is that we go backward in our growth or get stagnant and stuck. For the Christ-follower, whatever reason we choose to look at other people, if we take our eyes off Jesus, we no longer walk in freedom. In that case, religion wins and we don't live out our redemption.

You may be asking, "But, isn't religion supposed to be good?" Not when it focuses on rule-keeping and checking boxes for approval or disapproval. In attempting to be "good enough for God," we can become completely imprisoned by a checklist, driven solely by behavior. The dos and don'ts of the Ten Commandments weren't given to us so we would know how to be perfect every day. They were and are to show us that we desperately, constantly need God. We will never measure up to His holiness. We can't meet His standard, even on our best day.

But, our need *for* Him is also an invitation *from* Him to be fulfilled *in* Him. To live the life of the redeemed. Even back in the days of Jesus, religion falsely created a sort of sliding scale for people to think that some sins are worse than others.

That has always been a concept born out of religion—the opposite of walking free. Redemption comes when we accept the truth that, because of Jesus, we are forgiven for everything we have done, are doing, and will ever do. Period.

Our attitude of the heart then affects our perspective of the world, so when we look at the people around us, we don't compare ourselves. We don't compete. Instead, we walk committed to sharing the compassion and comfort of Christ. When we know Jesus is the Answer to save us from religion, we can walk freely through redemption.

Next-Step Questions

Why do you think we can so easily fall into religion by comparing ourselves to others instead of to God? How much have you struggled with this issue? Explain.

_____

_____

The depth of your prayer life is going to have a strong impact on living a redeemed life. What are some ways you can pray to focus on your own heart and life?

_____

_____

Setting aside religion for redemption, what is your one step of faith to take today?

_____

_____

God, help me to *STOP* looking at how bad anyone else is, and keep my eyes on how *GOOD* You are!

Retracing Your Steps

In my younger years, when I messed up in some way, I would let my mistakes beat me up, eat me up, and not let me up. That is, until I felt like I had punished myself enough to "pay for my sin." Until then, I would constantly think about what I had done wrong. I'd look back and so quickly be reminded of the shame I felt and focus on my pain—or the pain I had caused others. The stress and fear would hang in my chest like a weight.

But over time, I'm slowly gaining a better understanding. The closer I get to Jesus, the clearer the perspective I have when I look back on those same things. Why? Because I'm not looking at my mistakes from my point of view, but His. Because I'm closer to Him than I was before, I don't see my shame and pain the same anymore. Instead, I see more of His mercy and grace. I better see His invitation to freedom.

I am learning that if I ask Him, "God, can you change my circumstances?" and He says, "No," I can ask, "Then, can you change *me*, so I can handle the circumstances you're walking me through?"

From the countless people I have met across the country these past several years, I have found that the ones who feel the most discounted are those who have made mistakes they feel have disqualified them from God's grace. Or those who have had things done to them that make them feel unworthy. They believe they have somehow been ruined. Part of my message to those folks is the same one I have had to accept about myself: *Nothing* is beyond the reach of Jesus. No one is beyond His ability to save. No one has fallen further than His grace can grasp. There is no sin that mercy cannot cover.

Take a look back at your answers over the past six days and consider the decisions you have made to let go. Then commit to the following:

- Take a baby step and/or a bold step.
- Give up control and accept His comfort.
- Trade in your trinket for His treasure.
- Turn from spiritual blindness and toward belief.
- Transform your anxiety into His adventure.
- Repent of religiousness and accept a life redeemed.

Retracing Your Steps Questions

What was the easiest step for you to take this week?

_____

_____

RETRACING YOUR STEPS

What was the hardest step you took this week?

_____

_____

Name *all* the steps of faith you chose to take this week.

_____

_____

What can you carry out of this week into the rest of your life?

_____

_____

Responsible to Reconciled

No matter anyone's belief system, even agnosticism or atheism, we all understand that we are responsible for our own actions in this life. Even someone who does not believe in the concept of sin cannot deny personal accountability and consequences. When we do something wrong or harmful, someone has to take responsibility. So, we either take the weight of it all, or we try pushing it onto somebody else—whatever our choice, bearing all the responsibility for our wrongs can and will cripple us.

For this step, let's go all the way back to the beginning.

The serpent was the shrewdest of all the wild animals the Lord God had made. One day he asked the woman, "Did God really say you must not eat the fruit from any of the trees in the garden?"

"Of course, we may eat fruit from the trees in the garden," the woman replied. "It's only the fruit from the tree in the middle of the garden that we are not allowed to eat. God said, 'You must not eat it or even touch it; if you do, you will die.'"

"You won't die!" the serpent replied to the woman. "God knows that your eyes will be opened as soon as you eat it, and you will be like God, knowing both good and evil."

The woman was convinced. She saw that the tree was beautiful and its fruit looked delicious, and she wanted the wisdom it would give her. So she took some of the fruit and ate it. Then she gave some to her husband, who was with her, and he ate it, too. At that moment their eyes were opened, and they suddenly felt shame at their nakedness. So they sewed fig leaves together to cover themselves.

When the cool evening breezes were blowing, the man and his wife heard the LORD God walking about in the garden. So they hid from the LORD God among the trees. Then the LORD God called to the man, "Where are you?"

He replied, "I heard you walking in the garden, so I hid. I was afraid because I was naked."

"Who told you that you were naked?" the LORD God asked. "Have you eaten from the tree whose fruit I commanded you not to eat?" The man replied, "It was the woman you gave me who gave me the fruit, and I ate it."

Then the LORD God asked the woman, "What have you done?"

"The serpent deceived me," she replied. "That's why I ate it." (Genesis 3:1–13)

All the patterns of human behavior we rely on—and also suffer from—can be found in this passage. Let's look at them.

Misunderstanding (v. 3)

First, it is important to know that when God told Adam in Genesis 2:16–17, "You may freely eat the fruit of every tree in the garden—except the tree of the knowledge of good and evil. If you eat its fruit, you are sure to die," Eve had not yet been created. God made all the animal kingdom before creating her. So, how did she come to know the rule of the Garden? Did Adam tell her and get it wrong? Or did she just misunderstand when confronted by the serpent? Regardless, she added "and even touch it," which was never said.

Misunderstanding and miscommunication create and enhance sin all the time. We take too much or not enough responsibility because of these issues. And relationships break down over these two dynamics all the time. People remain estranged from each other for years, all based on bad info. Misunderstanding distracts from responsibility.

Lies (vv. 4–5)

This all started when the enemy misled and manipulated Eve. The serpent's goal was to convince Eve that God was keeping something from her. That He was hiding and withholding something valuable when, in reality, God was only protecting and providing for her. (Adam, however, did fail to protect her and then himself.) Every lie ever told since then has been based on these same principles of missing out on or misrepresenting the truth. Lies are an attempt to divert responsibility.

Hiding (v. 8)

From literal hiding to hiding our hearts to hiding the truth, this choice started here. Of course, while millions of people have attempted to hide from God, no one has ever been successful. He always knows who we are and where we are. Hiding is therefore just an attempt to avoid or delay responsibility.

Fear (v. 10)

Sin always evokes fear, and then fear usually causes more sin to follow. All fear is a response to knowing we must face responsibility.

Blame (vv. 12–13)

When God asked Adam to explain what happened, he avoided responsibility and blamed Eve. When God asked Eve, she avoided responsibility and blamed the serpent. While this is not in the passage, if God had asked the serpent to explain himself, he would likely have blamed God. Full circle. We must always remember: the enemy's fight has never been with us, but with God.

Responsibility for our sin never goes away. It remains until it's taken care of. But that is exactly why Jesus came to reconcile us. The easiest definition of *reconciliation* that I ever heard was that something was good, then it became bad, and then it was made good again. In the beginning, God created everything and said it was good, but then His human creation became bad. Jesus came so that we could be reconciled to God and be made good again.

Because of this, if we do not choose a relationship with God, we take full responsibility on our shoulders when we can just simply believe 1 Peter 5:7: "Give all your worries and cares to God, for he cares about you." Whatever is weighing on us, Jesus is the only safe place to cast our cares. Why? Because He cares deeply about the things that matter to us, all the struggles and challenges in our lives. So much that He gave His life for us.

On the cross, Christ took on the responsibility of our sin that we could not bear. Through His sacrifice, He created the opportunity for us to be reconciled to God. If we accept His offer, God then gives us the privilege of sharing His message with our circles of influence. A loving God we could never reach has come to offer us His life as we walk one reconciled step with Him at a time.

Next-Step Questions

Why do you think we tend to either take on the full burden of our own sin or want to blame others for our issues? Which do you tend to do?

_____

_____

How should an understanding of the forgiveness that comes from God's reconciliation affect our relationships with others?

_____

_____

Accepting reconciliation, what is your one step of faith to take today?

_____

_____

Sharing God's message
of reconciliation is not a
HAVE-TO,
but a *GET-TO*.

09

Hiding to Honesty

Yesterday, we talked about Adam and Eve trying to hide from God. We also talked about how we try to hide too—to avoid responsibility for our mistakes. In today's step, let's dive a little deeper into that concept.

So many people are convinced they are on this journey through life by themselves. Because of the isolation, they feel like they have to keep everything bottled up inside their hearts. Any struggles, pain, sickness, all the many ills of life, they try to carry alone. No wonder addiction, suicide, and violence are destroying so many every day. No wonder anxiety, depression, and desperation are rampant. That's plenty to try to hide from, right?

Jesus told us the truth about this world in John 16:33: "Here on earth you will have many trials and sorrows." In other words, we're all going to have to deal with the problems of this world. But He didn't stop there. The second part of the verse is: "But take heart, because I have overcome the world."

So, if Jesus has overcome the world and offers us His help, how can we stop the hiding? For me, I've found that the more honest I can be about my life—using wisdom and discretion, of course—the more I connect with people who have the same struggles that I do.

Now that we are into our second week, I want to encourage you to take a brave, bold, but very helpful and practical step. I want to invite you to reach out to someone you trust spiritually and tell that person how you are trying to walk in freedom right now. Try to find someone who is already walking that path or someone who is at least at the same place you are spiritually. One of the ways that Jesus helps us overcome the world is through sharing with one another. As He stated in Matthew 18:20, "For where two or three gather together as my followers, I am there among them."

With that in mind, let's talk about accountability from a spiritual perspective.

First, accountability is everywhere in our lives—laws, speed limits, tests, evaluations, job performance reviews, and so on. The point is to create or provide discipline and protection for society. This concept provides a framework under which we can all try to live with one another. For example, when you drive down the highway, the other person going in the opposite direction is holding you accountable to stay within the lines you have been provided. You are doing the same. If either of you breaks that trust and strays even a couple of feet, disaster occurs.

Our walk with Christ is very similar. Because of Him, accountability between two or more Christians can create a synergy, meaning the efforts together are greater than the individual parts. Sort of a 1 + 1 = 3 idea. Most people who work together in a team can always accomplish more than they can individually. That's especially true for us as Christ-followers.

> Two are better than one, because they have a good return for their labor: If either of them falls down, one can help the other up. But pity anyone who falls and has no one to help them up. . . . Though one may be overpowered, two can defend themselves. A cord of three strands is not quickly broken. (Ecclesiastes 4:9–10, 12 NIV)

Yet, even with this provision on our faith walk, we struggle to make use of it. Many people get together to talk and pray. Things go well at the start, but after a while, the meetings trail off. One of the biggest reasons is the people involved begin to see no purpose in getting together. Here's why that often happens: they practice *disclosure*, not *accountability*. *Disclosure* is simply sharing and confessing life details to one another, much like someone confesses to a pastor or priest. A minister can speak forgiveness and a prayer but doesn't require any other action from the person. Accountability is giving another person (or persons) permission to help you start or stop an action. With the intentional desire to change, you invite others to get into your business.

You may have heard of Alcoholics Anonymous. The organization has helped millions stop drinking by encouraging people to contact others who will help when temptation comes. It's not just about going to the meetings, but reaching out when you need help. Inviting intervention. That's the point of accountability.

For Christ-followers, confession and prayer are incredibly important ways to help one another grow and mature. But that's where the real help begins. We will face situations in our lives when we need some extra support for ongoing struggles. Accountability helps eliminate secrets, running, and hiding, bringing real honesty and transparency. It helps our private lives mirror our public lives. We have the best opportunity to become the same person alone that we are in a room of people we want to impress.

Maybe there is something you're hiding that is serious enough that you need to contact a pastor, priest, or professional counselor. Maybe that's the accountability you need to stop hiding—to get honest and find real help. But whether it's a professional or a trusted friend, if you're in this place, I encourage you to reach out and say, "I don't want to hide anymore. I want to stop being isolated. I really want to walk in freedom." Hiding will never bring freedom. Being honest first with yourself, second with God, and third with others is an incredible way to break the cycle of sin.

Considering our look at the serpent in the Garden yesterday, one of the consistent plays of the enemy is trying to convince us that we are the only person in the world who has ever battled the problem we have. He whispers accusations like, "Your friends don't struggle with this the way you do. If they knew about it, they would drop you like a rock." Or, "No one around you has to deal with this. Keep it to yourself, because they would never understand how bad you are." No matter how crazy that sounds, we can all fall into his lies.

To confess how our family was hurting because of Daniel's cancer or how we felt when our house was wrecked by a hurricane (more on that later) was difficult at first. I felt like the more I shared my hurt, the less perfect my life was, even though my life was *never* perfect. But, eventually, when I was able to share those feelings with others—when I started talking about it and confessing my hurts—I felt so much better. God began to teach me how to find hope in the midst of the helplessness. As I walked toward freedom, I refused to allow my struggles to wear me down and keep me from moving forward. I found comfort in knowing somebody else was aware of what I was going through and that I'd been feeling out of control in my life. And over time, after I'd gotten help to walk out of those feelings, I was even able to help lead others along that same path.

Accountability works best when, as you connect with someone on a deeper level, you both open up to a more meaningful relationship. I've found that a person showing me sympathy is good, but someone offering empathy is so much better. Sympathy is saying, "I've never dealt with what you're going through, but I'm so sorry and I'm here." Empathy is saying, "I've been through this, too, and I get it. I understand what you're walking through, and I'm here to tell you that you can get on the other side of this."

Being honest with someone who cares about you and then returning that favor on a two-way street is a game-changer.

In my relationships, the greatest speech anyone has ever given me had no words, only tears. Someone literally crying next to me with a hand on my shoulder spoke so much more than all the sermons I had ever heard. I have certainly walked alone, but now I know the freedom found in walking together with others who follow Christ. You can have those same kinds of relationships in your life.

> Is there any encouragement from belonging to Christ? Any comfort from his love? Any fellowship together in the Spirit? Are your hearts tender and compassionate? Then make me truly happy by agreeing wholeheartedly with each other, loving one another, and working together with one mind and purpose. (Philippians 2:1–2)

Next-Step Questions

Why do you think we come to believe that hiding is so much easier than being honest?

_____

_____

Who is a trusted friend (or friends) to whom you can reach out for help? Set a goal to contact that person in the next twenty-four hours and invite him or her into your journey.

_____

_____

What is your one step of faith to take today to end anything hidden and be as honest as possible?

_____

_____

Sometimes
the *BEST* speech
you can give has no words.

STEP

10

Pain to Progress

Everyone knows that working out to build muscle is going to require some physical pain. Pushing the body beyond discomfort is necessary to make *what*? Progress. The phrase "no pain, no gain" is still found in gyms all over the country.

The same is true for any sort of rehab or physical therapy after an injury or accident. Once the body is healed, pushing past any pain to regain mobility and agility is crucial.

As a youth pastor, I remember studying Bible commentaries to teach my students about Paul's thorn in the flesh, a very popular and intriguing passage where he talked about something painful in his life that God ultimately used to grow him. Here's what he wrote:

> To keep me from becoming proud, I was given a thorn in my flesh, a messenger from Satan to torment me and keep me from becoming proud.

Three different times I begged the Lord to take it away. Each time he said, "My grace is all you need. My power works best in weakness." So now I am glad to boast about my weaknesses, so that the power of Christ can work through me. That's why I take pleasure in my weaknesses, and in the insults, hardships, persecutions, and troubles that I suffer for Christ. For when I am weak, then I am strong. (2 Corinthians 12:7–10)

The "thorn in the flesh" is a reference to some sort of nagging problem that Paul had. Some theologians believe it could have been a literal splinter or burr in his skin that he couldn't pull out. Some believe that Paul had an actual physical ailment, an injury that wouldn't heal or a chronic problem that created constant pain for him.

Others believe it was his eyesight. After he was struck blind on the road to Damascus, maybe his vision was never fully restored. Paul's occasional reference to his own writing could have meant the actual size of the letters of the alphabet that he wrote to be able to see them clearly.

Another school of thought was the thorn might be one of the churches he had planted, like a constant problem child, so to speak. Every time he turned around, they messed up again and he was having to address them.

Regardless of what the source of pain may have been, Paul prayed three times specifically and fervently that God would free him from this pain. But he finally came to the conclusion that God was going to use the problem to progress him toward becoming more like Jesus. Paul believed God's decisions were for his best, never some sort of punishment or judgment. So whatever the problem was, he came to realize that he could no longer focus on his pain—a distraction that might keep him from taking the steps forward he needed to make.

Just as refusing to be active and exercise can eventually cause atrophy, spiritual atrophy is also possible. If we refuse to walk forward to grow and mature, we lose the progress we have made. Paul was determined not to make that mistake.

As we've said, in our daily walk with and in Christ, we will never be completely free of our hurts. But God uses our walk of faith toward Him to work out the pain in life. In those places, the more we trust Him, the closer we get to Him, and the more freedom we have, even in our pain. Like Paul stated, we can be made perfect in our weakness.

In John 15, Jesus spoke of spiritual pain that God initiates in our lives solely for us to be able to grow. In this passage, He called God the Gardener: "I am the true grapevine, and my Father is the gardener. He cuts off every branch of mine that doesn't produce fruit, and he prunes the branches that do bear fruit so they will produce even more" (vv. 1–2).

There are things in our lives that God has told us to get rid of—from toxic relationships to harmful habits to bad attitudes. When we refuse to hand those over, out of His great love, the Gardener may choose to remove them on His terms. That process will always be painful. But God in His wisdom has said, "Enough is enough. This has to go for you to be who I created you to be."

The great news is when we submit to God as our Gardener, new growth will take place. Because He alone knows where to cut, He knows what we need to grow. Most of us can look back in our lives at something God chose to remove and see now that was for the best. At the time, we would never have chosen that path, but today we are better for it.

A saying that many trainers repeat over and over to their athletes is, "Push past the pain." In the running world, it is often expressed as, "You have to hit the wall." The next time something painful is happening in your life, whether you volunteered for it or it was just suddenly cut off by the Gardener, remember that maturity and growth beyond where you have ever been is on the way. Never mistake a painful step as a wasted step. Anything that brings us closer to Jesus is always progress.

Next-Step Questions

What is the most painful experience you have ever had that you eventually saw was for your best? Explain.

_____

_____

How can you get better at reminding yourself about your spiritual progress whenever pain begins?

_____

_____

What is your one step of faith to take today in balancing your pain with spiritual progress?

_____

_____

We will **NEVER** fully
appreciate our progress
on the mountaintop
until we have **GROWN**
from our pain in the valley.

Compromise to Covered

Throughout our lives, we can quickly and easily end up in situations where we feel unsafe, unsteady, and unprotected. We can make decisions that leave us feeling naked and exposed, both emotionally and spiritually. Yet, in Christ, regardless of how we may feel in response to any circumstance, we remain under His covering.

Exactly what is that covering? Ephesians 2:13 states, "Once you were far away from God, but now you have been brought near to him through the blood of Christ." That means that on our best *and* worst days, we are covered by His sacrificial and redemptive blood shed on the cross.

So, when we deliberately choose to step out in sin, we refuse His covering.

One of the most complicated accounts of compromise found in Scripture involved David, the shepherd-turned-king who was amazingly close to God. Throughout his days, David was faithfully obedient to the Father. Those choices brought great favor on his life. But, just like Adam and Eve felt naked for the first time when they sinned, when David stepped out of the will of God, he also walked out from beneath his divine covering. God wanted to keep blessing him, but David forced Him to move to discipline. His care was still paternal, but the focus had to change due to the king's actions when he decided to step away from God's safety and security into a compromising position.

We know about David's sin with Bathsheba, but where did he *first* cross the line? Where did his compromise begin? Let's take a look.

> In the spring of the year, when kings normally go out to war, David sent Joab and the Israelite army to fight the Ammonites. They destroyed the Ammonite army and laid siege to the city of Rabbah. However, David stayed behind in Jerusalem. (2 Samuel 11:1)

After the winter thaw, kings were supposed to go out to battle with their armies. But, this particular year, David didn't. He decided to stay home and send his soldiers out without him. His first step of disobedience was not *being* what he was supposed to be (the warrior king) and not *doing* what he was supposed to do (ride out onto the battlefield, leading his men to fight). This seemingly harmless decision led to a domino effect that David would regret for the rest of his life.

> Late one afternoon, after his midday rest, David got out of bed and was walking on the roof of the palace.

As he looked out over the city, he noticed a woman of unusual beauty taking a bath. (2 Samuel 11:2)

Now, is there anything wrong with taking an afternoon nap? No, unless you're supposed to be somewhere important! Would David have taken a snooze on the battlefield? Likely not. Was he bored, home alone while all his buddies were out fighting? Sure sounds like it. But more important, when he should have been battling physical enemies, the spiritual enemy came to attack him.

Back to the story. After his private "peeping tom" session from his high vantage point, David called for Bathsheba to be brought to the palace. Even though he knew she was married, he slept with her. (For a woman in that day, refusing the king—even a good king—was not an option.) Later, when Bathsheba told David she was pregnant, he decided to try to cover his tracks with a conjugal visit from her husband, Uriah. But, even though Uriah returned on orders from the king, because of his strong loyalty to his fellow soldiers (David's own army) who were still on the battlefield, he refused to go home and be with his wife. David was desperate—he even tried to get Uriah drunk to better his chances.

When none of this worked, manipulation turned to assassination. David ordered that Uriah be placed on the front lines with no cover, sealing his fate. How do you suppose Bathsheba felt when she realized what David had done? How about everyone else? Each time the king made the next wrong move, the circle of people who saw his sin grew wider. From servants to soldiers, they would have easily seen what was actually going on.

Do you think David ever thought, *If only I had gone to war with my men? None of this would have ever happened!?* As they say, hindsight is always twenty-twenty. Today, having the entire story, we can trace it all back to that first moment when he compromised with a selfish decision.

Fast-forward to God calling Nathan the prophet to confront David. As king, he could have had Nathan executed for the confrontation. But David knew the message was actually from God and responded in brokenness and humility. The final chapter in this story is found in Psalm 51—David's plea for God to forgive his trail of sin and restore his covering. He was forced to view himself as a broken man, not a victorious king.

> Have mercy on me, O God,
>> because of your unfailing love.
> Because of your great compassion,
>> blot out the stain of my sins.
> Wash me clean from my guilt.
>> Purify me from my sin.
> For I recognize my rebellion;
>> it haunts me day and night. . . .
> You do not desire a sacrifice, or I would offer one.
>> You do not want a burnt offering.
> The sacrifice you desire is a broken spirit.
>> You will not reject a broken and repentant heart,
>> O God. (Psalm 51:1–3, 16–17)

The singular goal of our constant action steps in our walk of faith is to be obedient to the Lord. It's not about rules or a checklist, but being intentional to pray, "Today, I choose to take a step of obedience, because I want to keep the covering of Your will, along with the safety and security You bring." Christ died so that when we compromise, we can immediately ask forgiveness, make things right, and get right back under His covering. No wallowing. No wasting precious time. Just a step back into the freedom He has provided.

> He will cover you with his feathers.
> > He will shelter you with his wings.
> > His faithful promises are your armor and protection. (Psalm 91:4)

Next-Step Questions

What was your moment of greatest compromise, a time when you gave in to sin that cost you? Explain.

_____

_____

How did you resolve this experience with God, yourself, and others? Explain. (If you haven't resolved it yet, read through David's complete story for the pattern you, too, can follow: 2 Samuel 11–12 and Psalm 51.)

_____

_____

Avoiding compromise and living under God's covering, what is your one step of faith to take today?

_____

_____

To stay off the roof of
COMPROMISE,
we have to **LIVE** on
the altar of sacrifice.

STEP

12

Wondering to Wisdom

Over the course of our lives, we ask lots of questions about simple and ordinary things to complex and complicated matters. We wonder what we will become. Wonder who we will marry. Wonder what our kids will be like. Wonder how life will turn out at thirty, forty, and beyond. Wondering is simply wanting to know when we don't have a clue.

The other side of wondering is wisdom. If knowledge is learning a fact, then wisdom is much deeper and broader as the best application of anything we know. Wisdom is speaking and applying insight, good judgment, and discernment. While knowledge can be gained at *any* age, wisdom only comes *with* age and experience.

It's important that we remember that our own brand of worldly wisdom is much different from God's. He alone is the Author of truth, which also makes Him the Author of wisdom. Walking with Him is the only way to turn our wondering into real wisdom. We need that godly wisdom because it brings us a unique and eternal level of mental, emotional, and spiritual maturity.

In our wondering, does God give us some of the answers we want? Yes. All of them? No. But, for the questions He doesn't answer directly, He gives us tools and resources by which we can find the right answers. When God doesn't offer us the answer, it usually means He wants to teach us something during a season. And only He can determine how long that may last. But remember: the Christian life is not events, but a journey. There will be times when He doesn't give us answers, only more questions. This allows us to grow in qualities like patience and perseverance as we wait for wisdom.

The book of Proverbs talks about this throughout its pages, starting right out of the gate in chapter 1.

> Their purpose is to teach people wisdom and discipline,
>> to help them understand the insights of the wise.
> Their purpose is to teach people to live disciplined and successful lives,
>> to help them do what is right, just, and fair. (vv. 2–3)

I'm going to use a common analogy—one we all understand—about how we learn. When my kids were little and we would hang out in the kitchen as a family while dinner cooked, we would tell our son, "Don't touch the stove. It's hot."

He never touched it. Not once. He didn't have to get his own evidence of what we meant by hot. He stopped at "Don't touch."

When our daughter (who's a lot like me) got old enough to be mobile in the kitchen, we gave her the same warning. But, to her, it was more of a challenge than a caution. She wanted to blow past "Don't touch" and get straight to "What exactly do you mean by hot, and why is that a problem?" So, what finally cured her of trying to touch the stove? Actually touching the stove, then feeling the pain from the burn.

Both our kids gained wisdom about the heat of a stove. Our son learned through *instruction*. Our daughter learned through *experience*.

As the perfect Parent, the Lord knows what each of us needs at every stage of our lives, whether instruction or experience. He walks us through certain circumstances so that we may gain wisdom. *His* wisdom. *His* perspective. *His* view of any situation. That changes our worldview from wondering to seeing life through Him—the gaining of wisdom.

Now, let's go a little deeper: "If you need wisdom, ask our generous God, and he will give it to you. He will not rebuke you for asking" (James 1:5).

"If you need wisdom"? Wisdom about what? Well, for the answer, we have to go back to verses 2–4:

> Dear brothers and sisters, when troubles of any kind come your way, consider it an opportunity for great joy. For you know that when your faith is tested, your endurance has a chance to grow. So let it grow, for when your endurance is fully developed, you will be perfect and complete, needing nothing.

To paraphrase, "When troubles come, when your faith is tested, and you're wondering, 'What is going on and how can I get on the other side of this?' ask God to show you." Whether wisdom comes from a really hard step, a quick step, or a long-haul journey, His only goal is to teach us something so that we can move forward in and with Him.

I like to try new things, but it's hard for me to attempt something new if I don't think that I'll be good at it. I can spend too much time analyzing my success rate, for example, at a new hobby like golf or carpentry. I need to just pick up a golf club and go out onto a green or pull out a power tool and challenge a piece of wood. But, my fear of failing at something often keeps me from learning through trial and error, earning the experience required to get better. I can spend more time wondering than stepping out and putting in the hard work needed to gain wisdom. It's like if someone gave you a boat even though you've never sailed. While the safest place for the vessel is tied up in the harbor, that's not what boats are made for. They are built to set sail and go out into deep water. Jesus has given us the gift of being able to point our hearts toward the depth of wisdom and not settle for wondering in the shallows, playing it safe at the shoreline.

Wondering is built into our DNA. Throughout history, humans have looked to the stars and pondered, "What is beyond the sky?" They have looked to the seas and questioned, "What is beneath the surface?" Jesus invites us to follow after Him, far beyond our wondering, to a journey of faith that leads us into maturity and deep wisdom. With that assurance, we can take steps with confidence and joy.

Next-Step Questions

How do you typically handle and process the tough questions in your life? Explain.

_____

_____

What might need to change for you to better receive God's wisdom—His insight, discernment, and application of knowledge—in a deeper way than you ever have before?

_____

_____

What is your one step of faith to take today to gain more of God's wisdom?

_____

_____

KNOWLEDGE comes
one page at a time.
WISDOM comes
one day at a time.

Rebellious to Rebranded

Job descriptions, résumés, and titles are an important part of commerce and the marketplace. But when we take a realistic inventory of our personal lives, we find several roles, responsibilities, and expectations as well. In a career, at home, and in the community, we become known for certain things. A man can be a marketing director at work; a son, uncle, brother, husband, and dad to his family; a deacon in his church; a soccer coach for his kids; and a friend. A woman can be a CEO at her work; a daughter, aunt, sister, wife, and mother at home; a volunteer at her kids' school, and a friend. Within our households, we can have additional roles such as chef, chauffeur, and counselor as needs arise. Just thinking through and writing down the things that define us can be overwhelming. Yet, inside each of those positions an identity is projected for accomplishing the tasks. Different aspects of personality, comfort level, and social and cultural dynamics are necessary for each one.

Our faith in Christ creates some unique roles for us that affect eternity. While the majority of those roles won't make it to Heaven, Scripture does give us some clear titles and job descriptions. For example, in Matthew 25, when Jesus taught about being a loyal disciple, He used the phrase, "Well done, good and faithful servant." Countless sermons have used those words to describe what we all desire to hear one day. Regardless of any position we hold today, from career to family to community, as we stand before God, He will not say, "Well done, great teacher/amazing lawyer/awesome mom/incredible friend/fill in the blank." The only role that will count in that moment is "faithful servant."

But here's where today's step comes in. On our journey toward the day when we hear Jesus's greeting in Heaven, one thing always stands in our way: a rebellious heart. We're caught in the daily fight to serve not ourselves but Him and others. With so many of the earthly roles we pursue, climbing the ladder, beating out the competition, and winning is not only encouraged, but applauded. Our sin nature conditions us to have a "me first" response.

For this to change, we have to take on a new identity in Christ. This demands a rebranding. *Rebranding* is a marketing term for getting rid of an old, tired, often dying image to take on a new, fresh identity. But spiritually, we can't do that on our own. We fall short every time.

The only way to receive our true God-given rebrand is through the One who showed us how to escape rebellion and live a life of sacrifice. But, how does that happen?

> My old self has been crucified with Christ. It is no longer I who live, but Christ lives in me. So I live in this earthly body by trusting in the Son of God, who loved me and gave himself for me. (Galatians 2:20)

We cannot do it, but Christ can. When we try living on our own, we're going to be rebellious. But if we accept our identity in Him, He rebrands us to be even more than what we could ever be on our own. We surrender our old selves and invite Him to live His life and identity in us and through us.

Once we start to live out this rebranded life, another new role comes into play:

> This means that anyone who belongs to Christ has become a new person. The old life is gone; a new life has begun!
>
> And all of this is a gift from God, who brought us back to himself through Christ. And God has given us this task of reconciling people to him. For God was in Christ, reconciling the world to himself, no longer counting people's sins against them. And he gave us this wonderful message of reconciliation. So we are Christ's ambassadors; God is making his appeal through us. We speak for Christ when we plead, "Come back to God!" For God made Christ, who never sinned, to be the offering for our sin,

so that we could be made right with God through Christ. (2 Corinthians 5:17–21)

God has given us a job description that overrides all others. Even out of our rebellion, whether we feel worthy, qualified, or deserving of this, He has called each of us to be His

- ambassadors
- messengers of reconciliation
- representatives of righteousness

To live as a faithful servant who walks through life as Christ's ambassador, this calling needs to change the way we approach all the other titles, roles, and responsibilities we have. Why? Because at our jobs, in our homes, in the community, and even at church, we no longer represent ourselves, but Christ. It's no longer our message to get across, but His. It's no longer about our performance, but rather submitting to Him to work through us. With this as our overarching role in life, the freedom can be amazing. "I no longer live, but Christ in me." This rebranded identity overcomes our rebellious hearts, defining and affecting everything.

To be clear, an ambassador is a messenger who speaks for a higher authority. When we follow Christ, we also become God's ambassadors and then take the new role into every aspect of our world. So if we take that step today, we are saying, "I don't identify any longer with the way I want to go. It's about choosing to line up with Jesus, who lives within me." The amazing thing about making this choice is we will inevitably become better spouses, parents, employers, employees, friends, and all the other roles we have here on earth.

As we finish today's journey, I want to repeat Galatians 2:20, this time from The Message Bible, a great expression of this passage.

> Indeed, I have been crucified with Christ. My ego is no longer central. It is no longer important that I appear righteous before you or have your good opinion, and I am no longer driven to impress God. Christ lives in me. The life you see me living is not "mine," but it is lived by faith in the Son of God, who loved me and gave himself for me. I am not going to go back on that.

Next-Step Questions

What are the areas of your life where you continue to struggle with rebelling against authority, including God's? Explain.

_____

_____

How can the truth of Galatians 2:20 and 2 Corinthians 5:17–21 help you rethink and restructure your identity, your approach to life, and all your roles and responsibilities?

_____

_____

What is your one step of faith to take today to walk from places of rebellion to His rebranding?

_____

_____

There are **ALWAYS**
two choices in life:
rebel from God or
RUN to Him.

_____

Retracing Your Steps

A very difficult truth to accept, especially in Western culture, is that God cares more about making us holy than making us happy. But even a cursory glance through Scripture at the Old Testament prophets and New Testament apostles proves this to be true. Their circumstances were often difficult for a greater purpose. The same can be said for us.

Of course, God wants us to be happy. But the point is that happiness is often not His ultimate goal. For us to grow, to change, to mature in a fallen world, happiness often must take a back seat to the transformation in holiness. The more holiness He produces in us, the more joy we will experience. Joy in the soul beats any temporary happiness on this earth. A great meal, a good book, a hug from your child, or a job bonus can make us happy. But those things will soon fade, while the joy of Christ produced out of holiness will last over any temporary circumstance.

In John 17, before He went to the cross, Jesus prayed:

Make them holy by your truth; teach them your word, which is truth. Just as you sent me into the world, I am sending them into the world. And I give myself as a holy sacrifice for them so they can be made holy by your truth. (vv. 17–19)

Happiness is	Holiness is
• dependent on current circumstances	• dependent on eternal circumstances
• in the moment	• in the long haul
• a feeling that comes and goes	• a quality that never leaves

Here's the beautiful thing: with every step—even the difficult ones—we take toward holiness, we discover that nothing will bring us more joy. It's not like we have to choose one over the other. If we take the path of happiness, we will not always find holiness, but if we pursue holiness, it will always produce joy.

What joy for those you choose to bring near,
those who live in your holy courts. (Psalm 65:4)

For the Kingdom of God is not a matter of what we eat or drink, but of living a life of goodness and peace and joy in the Holy Spirit. (Romans 14:17)

Many things in this life can make us happy. But only one thing can make us holy: a relationship with God through

Christ. And when we allow the Spirit to make us holy, the fruit of that relationship is joy, goodness, and peace. Wouldn't a person who displays these qualities most likely be a happy person? I'm thinking yes.

As you review our journey over the past six days, I'm sure you're realizing that a lot of the concepts we've talked about are hard to live out. Surrendering to Jesus and handing over our flesh, sin, and personal agendas is a tough choice to make. But, today, keep this in mind: the goal is your personal holiness—becoming more and more like Jesus as you walk with Him in freedom.

Take some time to review your answers from Steps 8 through 13, looking at how you are going to step away from the following:

- taking responsibility for the burden of your own sin and instead moving toward reconciliation
- moving from hiding into honesty
- accepting pain to see progress
- compromising to be under His covering
- wondering into His wisdom
- walking away from rebellion to pursue His rebranding

Retracing Your Steps Questions

What was the easiest step for you to take this week?

_____

_____

What was the hardest step you took this week?

_____

_____

Name *all* the steps of faith you chose to take this week.

_____

_____

What can you carry out of this week into the rest of your life?

_____

_____

STEP

15

Victim to Victor

If any person in the Bible reflects the constant journey of choosing the role of victor over victim, it's Joseph in the Old Testament. Let's walk through his story, step by step. (Even if you feel like you know this account well, dig in and take a fresh look. One of the many beautiful aspects of Scripture is that each reading can bring a new perspective or lesson.)

In Genesis 37, the story begins with Joseph at around seventeen years old, working for his older half-brothers. Joseph was their father Jacob's favorite. To show his deep love for his youngest, one day Jacob presented Joseph with a beautiful robe—which of course made his brothers jealous. Add to that the frustration of Joseph sharing some prophetic dreams of how one day his brothers would bow down to him, and they decided they'd had enough of their little brother.

When Jacob sent Joseph to check on his brothers out in the field, they decided to use the opportunity to their advantage. As they watched Joseph coming toward them, they debated how to take him out. Some wanted to kill him and tell Dad a wild animal had attacked him. But in the end they decided to throw him into an empty well and leave him there to die—actually a much worse death than just killing him on the spot.

While they were debating, a money-making opportunity happened by.

> Then, just as they were sitting down to eat, they looked up and saw a caravan of camels in the distance coming toward them. It was a group of Ishmaelite traders taking a load of gum, balm, and aromatic resin from Gilead down to Egypt. . . . So when the Ishmaelites, who were Midianite traders, came by, Joseph's brothers pulled him out of the cistern and sold him to them for twenty pieces of silver. And the traders took him to Egypt. (Genesis 37:25, 28)

Imagine for a moment Joseph being led away, hands tied, watching his bitter, jealous brothers disappear into the distance, knowing not even one of them would come to his defense. Would this be an easy opportunity to turn his back on God, write off his family, hate life, and become a victim? Absolutely.

Once in Egypt, the traders sold Joseph to Potiphar, captain of Pharaoh's palace guard. Potiphar quickly realized the young man had something special about him, so he promoted Joseph to oversee his entire household. But Potiphar's wife also took notice in a much different way and decided to seduce him. When Joseph's integrity and faithfulness to God caused him to refuse her, she decided to get revenge by falsely charging Joseph with attempted rape. Potiphar believed her, or at least wouldn't go against her, and demanded Joseph be sent to prison.

Here we go again. Wouldn't this be an easy opportunity for Joseph to turn his back on God, write off any authority, hate life, and become a victim? For sure. But to no one's surprise, in prison Joseph became the warden's favorite and, just as happened at Potiphar's house, was put in charge of everything.

It's time to stop here and offer the reason why Joseph kept being promoted, no matter where he was placed: "The LORD was with him and caused everything he did to succeed" (Genesis 39:23).

In other words, God was in control of everything that had happened to Joseph and had a purpose for all of it. And it wasn't to be a victim.

While in prison Joseph successfully interpreted the dreams of some of Pharaoh's staff who had also been put behind bars. At least two years later, after word finally got back to the nation's leader about this gift, Pharaoh sent for Joseph. He successfully interpreted Pharoah's dream, making it clear that God was the One providing the prophecy. At the end of his explanation, Joseph said, "Therefore, Pharaoh should find an intelligent and wise man and put him in charge of the entire land of Egypt" (Genesis 41:33). Then this happened:

> So Pharaoh asked his officials, "Can we find anyone
> else like this man so obviously filled with the spirit of
> God?" Then Pharaoh said to Joseph, "Since God has

revealed the meaning of the dreams to you, clearly no one else is as intelligent or wise as you are. You will be in charge of my court, and all my people will take orders from you. Only I, sitting on my throne, will have a rank higher than yours." (Genesis 41:38–40)

Now, think about the many traumatic events in Joseph's life. None of it was a consequence of his sin. It was just the result of dealing with very selfish, sometimes evil people. Safe to say, after being sold into slavery by his family, falsely accused of attempted rape, thrown in prison under bogus charges, having people break their promises, resulting in years of imprisonment, most people would be bitter, angry, or even violent. But Joseph chose God's way every time, and God took care of him every time. By the end of the story, Joseph had saved his entire family and moved them into his home. Even when he had the position and power to have all his brothers enslaved or killed, he chose forgiveness, reconciliation, and redemption. Each time, he chose victory, as if becoming a victim of his circumstances wasn't even an option for him.

One of the many reasons this account is in the Bible is to show us God's way out of tragedy after tragedy, out of unfair circumstances, out of choosing our way or the world's way. As we walk through our own challenges, Joseph's story needs to be a constant reminder and promise to us that faithfulness to God will, ultimately, win out. Even when our circumstances make us feel like He has abandoned us, that is only a temporary state in an eternal relationship. We never have to be anyone's victim when we can choose the victory through Christ.

Next-Step Questions

Have any circumstances occurred in your life that made you feel like a victim? Explain.

_____

_____

Has your relationship with God changed any tragic circumstances into victory? (If you are still battling the role of victim, using Joseph's story, how might a relationship with God change your view of the struggles?)

_____

_____

Rejecting victimization and receiving God's victory, what is your one step of faith to take today?

_____

_____

We can become
CRIPPLED as victims
or allow God to *CREATE*
our victory.

16

Crippled to Carried

Yesterday, we closed by using the word *crippled* in terms of being a victim—accepting that a state of mind can be crippling to us, mentally, emotionally, or spiritually. Transitioning from that theme, today we're going to look at another Old Testament story that centers around a guy with one of the toughest names to pronounce in the entire Bible—Mephibosheth (*Meh-fi-bo-sheth*). (Saying that three times fast is nearly impossible. You're trying it right now, aren't you?) Mephibosheth was King Saul's grandson and Jonathan's son. Jonathan was David's best friend.

To begin, 2 Samuel 4:4 tells us that when the news came that Saul and Jonathan had been killed in battle when Mephibosheth was five years old, his nurse picked him up to flee in fear of someone coming to kill them. But she dropped him, causing some sort of permanent injury. Obviously, someone with any sort of disability in those days would have a very difficult and challenging life.

How does Mephibosheth's back story relate to today's theme? Well, after David became king, because of his deep friendship with Jonathan, he asked,

> "Is anyone in Saul's family still alive—anyone to whom I can show kindness for Jonathan's sake?" He summoned a man named Ziba, who had been one of Saul's servants. . . .
>
> The king then asked him, "Is anyone still alive from Saul's family? If so, I want to show God's kindness to them."
>
> Ziba replied, "Yes, one of Jonathan's sons is still alive. He is crippled in both feet."
>
> "Where is he?" the king asked.
>
> "In Lo-debar," Ziba told him, "at the home of Makir son of Ammiel."
>
> So David sent for him. (2 Samuel 9:1–2, 3–5)

An important side note to this story is that a common practice for new kings was to locate any relatives of the old king. The point was to eliminate *anyone* who might try to make a claim for the throne. (In Matthew 2, Herod wanted Jesus found and killed as a child so He would not grow up to be a threat.) Evil, insecure kings wanted to take out any potential competition from the old regime.

Even though David was not like that at all, we can't know for certain if Mephibosheth ever knew of his dad's close relationship with David. So, it is very possible that when the king's servants showed up to take him back to the palace, he assumed his death was near—or, at best, that he would be kept alive in prison or slavery. Even the village where Mephibosheth lived was in the middle of nowhere, as if he might have not just been poor, but hiding out.

Living in a day with no wheelchairs or other resources, a crippled person would have had to crawl or be carried anywhere. So, once they returned, the king's servants would have had to carry Mephibosheth in to place him before David. Imagine Mephibosheth's embarrassment, humiliation, and fear when he was literally set down before the king. He could have easily assumed the worst was about to happen. But take a look at this:

> When he came to David, he bowed low to the ground in deep respect. David said, "Greetings, Mephibosheth."
>
> Mephibosheth replied, "I am your servant."
>
> "Don't be afraid!" David said. "I intend to show kindness to you because of my promise to your father, Jonathan. I will give you all the property that once belonged to your grandfather Saul, and you will eat here with me at the king's table!"
>
> Mephibosheth bowed respectfully and exclaimed, "Who is your servant, that you should show such kindness to a dead dog like me?" (2 Samuel 9:6–8)

Check out David's response, as he ignored Mephibosheth's self-deprecating question:

> Then the king summoned Saul's servant Ziba and said, "I have given your master's grandson everything that belonged to Saul and his family. You and

your sons and servants are to farm the land for him
to produce food for your master's household. But
Mephibosheth, your master's grandson, will eat here
at my table." (Ziba had fifteen sons and twenty servants.) (2 Samuel 9:9–10)

Not death but a brand-new life was waiting for
Mephibosheth. Not prison or slavery or any form of punishment, but incredible blessing beyond his wildest dreams.
When David invited him to his table, he was immediately
freed from every fear and worry. His future was secured by
what would equate to the king's adoption, protection, and
provision for the rest of his life.

This Old Testament account is an incredible parable of
our own lives. From a spiritual perspective, we are all like
Mephibosheth, and King David represents what Jesus provides for us. We are all crippled by sin, pain, struggles, problems, issues, and scars, making us feel fearful and unworthy
to stand before a holy God. To have a permanent seat at
Jesus's banquet table, we must first acknowledge Him as
Lord to establish a relationship, just like Mephibosheth had
to face David. In our fallen state, Christ has to carry us to
His table. But, He has promised us there is a place for each of
us there, *if* we choose to accept, regardless of how crippled
we may be.

Walking in freedom does not mean we have to be fully
healed. Every time my brother has battled cancer, he has
made it through all the trauma and pain in total freedom.
Every time I step onto a stage, I am not anywhere close to
perfect, but I am free. In Christ, we aren't dependent on any

personal or external circumstances, because the liberty is in our spirits, our hearts, our souls. Freedom is not found in the absence of anything, but in the presence of Jesus.

Even when we have to be carried to make a step, whether suffering a physical ailment, a mental struggle, or an emotional issue, we are invited to dine alongside all the other coheirs in Christ—all those like us who are also crippled in different ways.

The name Mephibosheth actually means "dispeller of shame." He was given that name years before he was dropped and crippled. But his name ultimately reflected his heart and a prophecy of his life. The sins of his grandfather Saul would no longer determine his reputation, because the new king had reconciled the past and brought him to his table.

Here's one last point to consider about our step today. Once someone crippled is seated at a table, no one can tell the difference between that person and anyone else. Once seated, we all look the same. Before Jesus, we are all equal in our sin. After Jesus, we are all equal in our salvation. That's what happens when we are carried to the Lord's table.

Next-Step Questions

Has there been or is there something in your life, known or unknown to others, that has crippled you? Explain.

_____

_____

How did or how has your relationship with Christ affected whatever crippled you? (If you are still in the struggle of feeling crippled, using Mephibosheth's story with David, how might your relationship with God change the view of your battle?)

_____

_____

What is your one step of faith to take today in acknowledging being crippled and allowing God to carry you?

_____

_____

A seat at Jesus's table
PROVIDES
community, comfort, and
COMPASSION.

STEP

17

Conflicted to Connected

After reading the New Testament, you can easily see the vast difference in how Peter's life ended up versus Judas's. But, in those early days with Jesus, would anyone have been able to predict the outcome of these men? Likely not. In fact, a lot of people might have chosen Judas over the aggressive, loud, quick-tempered fisherman named Peter.

So, let's take a look at the difference between these two disciples. They began to follow Christ at around the same time. They started off their journey with Jesus with the same opportunity on the same level; both were given responsibility in His ministry. The only difference seemed to be that Jesus would invite Peter, James, and John into situations that didn't include the others. So did that create jealousy with Judas? We don't know.

But just before the crucifixion, Peter's and Judas's lives took very dramatic turns. Seemingly out of nowhere, we find this:

> Then Judas Iscariot, one of the twelve disciples, went to the leading priests and asked, "How much will you pay me to betray Jesus to you?" And they gave him thirty pieces of silver. From that time on, Judas began looking for an opportunity to betray Jesus. (Matthew 26:14–16)

Now, Judas didn't just suddenly get the idea to betray Jesus. There had to have been moments along the way when he was conflicted but finally gave in to the thoughts and decided to act on them. Whatever the case that brought him to this point, Judas completed his betrayal of Christ in the Garden of Gethsemane.

While Judas took the offense by leading the soldiers to Jesus, Peter jumped into defensive mode between the Lord and the mob by swinging a sword. In that moment, cowardice and bravery clearly separated the two men. But in the courtyard near the trials later that night, Peter joined Judas's betrayal through his three prophesied denials.

Yet, even while he distanced himself from Jesus to save his own skin, we have to give Peter some credit for being the closest one to the Lord. And, in fact, in just a matter of days, Peter began his journey to becoming the rock of the church, while Judas took his own life in shame, guilt, and regret.

So, what in the world happened? What caused one man to take such a different road than the other when they had been on what appeared to be equal ground for several years?

In general, what causes two people to accept Christ at around the same time, but while one becomes a spiritual leader the other fades into the status quo?

If you believe God gives us free will to make choices about Him and that Jesus came to offer everyone the same opportunity to know Him, the bottom line is that some folks take Him up on His offer and some don't. Some struggle with being conflicted while others get connected. Scripture tells us in several places that some will appear to be followers, but in the end it will be seen that they are not. The outward view may appear very spiritual, but in reality the person is not at all.

It's true that because of our sin, we are all conflicted about matters of faith. But once we come to know Christ, we either become more and more connected to Him or we allow other conflicts to come in to create doubts and questions. The choice between Judas and Peter is always there for any of us.

The Message Bible has an interesting take on Jesus talking about this subject in Matthew 7:21–23:

> Knowing the correct password—saying "Master, Master," for instance—isn't going to get you anywhere with me. What is required is serious obedience—*doing* what my Father wills. I can see it now—at the Final Judgment thousands strutting up to me and saying, "Master, we preached the Message, we bashed the demons, our super-spiritual projects had everyone talking." And do you know what I am going to say? "You missed the boat. All you did was use me to make yourselves important. You don't impress me one bit. You're out of here."

Preaching, bashing demons, and leading super-spiritual projects are all evidence of belief, yet Jesus said that doesn't get you the key to His Kingdom. In fact, He shows that person the door. So, how can we stay connected?

> Anyone who listens to my teaching and follows it is wise, like a person who builds a house on solid rock. Though the rain comes in torrents and the floodwaters rise and the winds beat against that house, it won't collapse because it is built on bedrock. But anyone who hears my teaching and doesn't obey it is foolish, like a person who builds a house on sand. When the rains and floods come and the winds beat against that house, it will collapse with a mighty crash. (Matthew 7:24–27)

The person who is known as wise, whose house survives, and who is a citizen in the Kingdom of God does two things.

1. *Hears Jesus's words.* We hear all the time, but that is no guarantee that we listen. In fact, proactive listening in this culture is a dying art. So when Jesus speaks to us, we must hear *and* listen and take in exactly what He is saying.

2. *Put Jesus's words into practice.* Practice like a doctor or lawyer, not a sports team. We're not getting *ready* for the big game; we are *in* the big game. We put Jesus's words into action in our lives. He tells us something we did not know or did not yet know to do, and then we put those words into practice. We apply His words. We obey His instruction. We take action in His name.

The difference between Peter and Judas ended up being the willingness to listen and obey. One thing is for sure—regardless of who we are, our background or belief, we are all serving and worshiping something. We will either take the uncertain road of disobedience or the redemptive path that keeps us connected to Christ.

Next-Step Questions

What are your strongest conflicted questions and doubts about your faith? Explain.

_____

_____

How can listening daily to Jesus's voice through the power of the Holy Spirit keep you connected and resolve your conflicts?

_____

_____

What is your one step of faith to take today in addressing conflicts of faith and staying connected to Christ?

_____

_____

NO ONE can
dispute, debate,
or disagree with a
changed ***HEART***.

Earthly to Eternal

The author of the book of Hebrews wrote, "For this world is not our permanent home; we are looking forward to a home yet to come" (13:14). In Philippians 3:20–21, Paul stated,

> But we are citizens of heaven, where the Lord Jesus Christ lives. And we are eagerly waiting for him to return as our Savior. He will take our weak mortal bodies and change them into glorious bodies like his own, using the same power with which he will bring everything under his control.

Once we enter a relationship with Jesus, we are promised a home in Heaven, making this world no longer our place of citizenship. That will not come until we step into eternity. Meanwhile, we have to keep dealing with the "stuff of earth": "So we don't look at the troubles we can see now; rather, we fix our gaze on things that cannot be seen. For the things we see now will soon be gone, but the things we cannot see will last forever" (2 Corinthians 4:18).

Now, let's get real. We can believe our new home is in Heaven and not here. That sounds great. But finances, pressures, sickness, and all our many problems are in our face all the time. It's a tough step to take when we promise not to look at those troubles, but to "fix our gaze" on Jesus, someone we cannot yet see. After accepting Christ, we usually want a change of scenery from our old life as we begin our new one of obedience. But, the majority of the time, what we see every day does not change. We must allow Jesus to change *us* in the midst of the troubles, problems, and our same ol', same ol' scenery. We have to change our mindset.

How can we do that? Well, while thousands and thousands of theologians have offered countless interpretations of the Sermon on the Mount, here is one very simple and practical version, using the mountain as a visual image of our spiritual journey.

- *"Blessed are the poor in spirit, for theirs is the kingdom of heaven" (Matthew 5:3 NIV).* "Poor in spirit" means a bankrupt state in our souls. We have nothing of value and no way to pay our debt of sin. Therefore, we are in great need.
- *"Blessed are those who mourn, for they will be comforted" (Matthew 5:4 NIV).* Realizing there is no way to meet that need, we now mourn our state of fallenness, recognizing the destitute and desperate condition of our hearts.
- *"Blessed are the meek, for they will inherit the earth" (Matthew 5:5 NIV).* Meekness or submission comes

out of humility after understanding both our need and our sin.

- *"Blessed are those who hunger and thirst for righteousness, for they will be filled" (Matthew 5:6 NIV).* Because of our bankrupt state, we hunger and thirst for something greater than ourselves.
- *"Blessed are the merciful, for they will be shown mercy" (Matthew 5:7 NIV).* Then comes God's provision to meet our needs. He fills us with blessing, making us fully satisfied. We then become merciful, for we have received great mercy.
- *"Blessed are the pure in heart, for they will see God" (Matthew 5:8 NIV).* The mercy we receive brings purity to the heart, allowing us to experience the presence of God.
- *"Blessed are the peacemakers, for they will be called children of God" (Matthew 5:9 NIV).* And, finally, we become advocates, ambassadors, and peacemakers for God as we now understand and submit to a relationship with Him.

In the journey through Jesus's Beatitudes, we started out in the valley and came up the mountain in verses 3, 4, and 5; reached the summit in verse 6; and then came down the other side as a new person in verses 7, 8, and 9 to share His peace with others.

When you realize you are poor in spirit—totally dependent on God—you then become merciful to others. When you mourn over the impure state of your heart, then and only then can your heart be cleansed and purified by God's power. Meekness will reign in the heart and life of a peacemaker.

No matter our current circumstances on earth, we know that Heaven has something far better in store for us. And, even here, we have a common denominator with Heaven—Jesus's presence. The Holy Spirit is with us right now, giving us insight, direction, gifts, and instructions that are better than anything we can physically see. So, as we take a step from earth to the eternal, it may not change the scenery around us, but Jesus can change us to fit Heaven inside the scenery. What problems are weighing you down today? What are you struggling with regarding the issues on this earth that need an eternal perspective? Know that God always offers you His perspective to see things from a better view and a more hopeful place.

Next-Step Questions

Do you think most of the people around you are growing tired of the things of this earth? Explain.

_____

_____

How is the desperate condition of life on earth making it easier to consider the reality of Heaven?

_____

_____

What is your one step of faith to take today in focusing on the eternal, not the things of this earth?

_____

_____

Focus on the reality of
HEAVEN,
not the wreckage on
EARTH.

Test to Testimony

See if this sounds familiar. It's a Monday morning and, as you look at your week, it's not too bad. Fairly normal, you think. But then by around 11:00 a.m., life has hit the fan. Everything has been changed by a major crisis. Suddenly, your normal week is shot, and you find yourself stressed out, trying to figure out what to do to just survive the day.

As Christ-followers, we have to keep in mind that anything entering our lives has to come through the hands of God. While He doesn't cause these challenges, He is never surprised by what happens, and He allows those circumstances into our lives. A quote repeated by countless people is that God does not test us to see what we are made of, because He already knows. He tests us so that *we* can see what we are made of. And, most important, so we can understand that we desperately need Him.

When we face any crisis, small or large, we must first realize it's a test and then, second, know that on the other side we need to discover the point of and the purpose for what happened to us. Why? Because any test can become a testimony—a story to share with others about what God has done in our lives.

One of the greatest tests in Scripture is found in the story of Abraham and Isaac. God's promise to Abraham had come true, and his wife, Sarah, had a son, Isaac. But then, when the boy was older, God told Abraham to take his son up to the mountain and offer him as a sacrifice.

Now, think for a moment how this command would not make any sense to Abraham. God had told him he would be the father of a great nation as vast as the stars in the sky. Abraham finally had the son who could begin the promised legacy. But then God told him to sacrifice the boy. Here's how the dreaded day started:

> The next morning Abraham got up early. He saddled his donkey and took two of his servants with him, along with his son, Isaac. Then he chopped wood for a fire for a burnt offering and set out for the place God had told him about. (Genesis 22:3)

Apparently, Abraham didn't put up a fight with God. Instead, he expressed incredible faith by just obeying. He placed the wood for the sacrifice on Isaac's shoulders—a definite foreshadowing of Christ carrying the cross on His shoulders to Calvary. And on the way up, as Isaac took inventory and pointed out to his dad that they had the wood and the fire but no lamb, Abraham assured his son that God would provide what was needed.

Once they arrived at the top, things got really intense for both father and son.

> When they arrived at the place where God had told him to go, Abraham built an altar and arranged the wood on it. Then he tied his son, Isaac, and laid him on the altar on top of the wood. And Abraham picked up the knife to kill his son as a sacrifice. At that moment the angel of the LORD called to him from heaven, "Abraham! Abraham!"
>
> "Yes," Abraham replied. "Here I am!"
>
> "Don't lay a hand on the boy!" the angel said. "Do not hurt him in any way, for now I know that you truly fear God. You have not withheld from me even your son, your only son."
>
> Then Abraham looked up and saw a ram caught by its horns in a thicket. So he took the ram and sacrificed it as a burnt offering in place of his son. (Genesis 22:9–13)

Remembering that they were just normal people like us, we have to think about the horror of this moment for Abraham and the terror that Isaac must have felt when he realized what his dad was doing. The test came to a fever pitch when Abraham raised the knife. But the point of greatest faith was also the complete passing of the test. The "angel of the Lord," who some theologians believe is a reference to Jesus, called for Abraham to stop at the last second. Isaac was then replaced by a ram.

To again connect this to Christ, He was not spared at the last second like Isaac. No ram was given to replace Him. In fact, His death was offered as a sacrifice to replace ours. Christ was God's final provision for the redemption of our sin.

To pass the test, Abraham had to place more faith in God than he ever had before and then be willing to sacrifice everything to experience a far deeper level of relationship with Him. For his obedience, he didn't become wealthy or powerful or gain any other kind of immediate material blessing. What He did receive, however, was much bigger: the beginning of a new relationship with His God and his son. And the establishment of multiple generations of men—Abraham, Isaac, and Jacob—who will forever represent God's plan for His people.

In His own way, God will bring His challenge of sacrifice into our lives as well. He will see if we will go to the mountain and set up the altar. But here is a major teaching point that we cannot miss with this step: God doesn't always provide a ram to replace the things He calls us to sacrifice to Him. There are times when He knows the best thing for our lives, both now and in the future, is for us to hand over what He has asked for. To be clear, that will never involve someone's death, just like it didn't in Abraham's and Isaac's story. But it might be a relationship, job, title, role, or place. And we must be willing to give it up.

We usually can't see the full outcome of our sacrifice. We likely won't understand what He is doing or why. But we have to come to a place of accepting that if God asks us to give something up to Him, it will ultimately be for our best. Whether He provides the "ram" or causes us to go through with our sacrifice, we have to trust that we will eventually see the point and the purpose for our test so that it can become our testimony one step at a time.

Next-Step Questions

What is the greatest spiritual test you have experienced where you knew God was asking you to sacrifice? Explain.

_____

_____

What was the testimony that God formed through your obedience? (If you are in the midst of that sacrifice now, what do you believe God is showing you, and what do you hope to see?)

_____

_____

Accepting that all tests can become testimonies, what is your one step of faith to take today?

_____

_____

The *PATH* to any testimony will always *START* with a test.

20

Misery to Mission

A t church or any Christian organization, we can always find volunteer positions in which we can "do ministry." We can find places to plug in and serve. For example, when a church needs volunteers for the nursery on Sunday morning, they don't announce, "If anyone believes God has called them to the nursery ministry, please let us know." No, that message usually goes, "We need people to help us in the church nursery this morning." This is just one of the many examples in and around the weekly operations of the church where we see this dynamic play out.

But anytime God Himself calls us to a mission where we will create ministry, that is a very different circumstance. In my own life, there was a point when I knew I was called to be a youth pastor and served in the church for several years. Then I was led away from that role and mission into a music ministry, where I am today. But my wife and I know that God has the absolute right any time down the road to call me into something else. Of course, my family has always been and will always be a major part of that commitment. Because He is our God, He gets to call the shots on what we do and where we go. To me, my calling into music isn't any more or less important than my calling to be a youth pastor.

But most often, as we talked about yesterday, God will get us ready for what He calls us to do by putting us through some tests. For most of us, that will involve going through some difficult circumstances and, yes, some misery. I recall a time early on in my music journey when I was stuck in California alone on a tour bus parked in a parking lot for three days with no air conditioning. I couldn't afford to fly home, so I had to wait for the bus to leave. I only had a twenty-dollar bill to buy food. My wife had called me to say, "Don't spend any money because we only have eighty-seven cents in our bank account."

Had God called me to do music for Him? Yes. Did my wife agree with the calling? Yes. Was being broke and alone and hot, four states apart, a miserable place for us? I can tell you, for sure, it absolutely was.

As we noted earlier, following Jesus's baptism, the Holy Spirit led Him into the wilderness alone. Why? Matthew 4:1 states, "to be tempted there by the devil." After fasting for forty days and nights, Satan came to Him. Was that a miserable place for Jesus to be? Let's see—hot, thirsty, dirty, exhausted, and then His archenemy showed up. Yeah, that's miserable, all right.

Let's take a closer look at the story.

Temptation #1

During that time the devil came and said to him, "If you are the Son of God, tell these stones to become loaves of bread."

But Jesus told him, "No! The Scriptures say,
'People do not live by bread alone,
   but by every word that comes from the mouth of God.'" (Matthew 4:3–4)

Notice the deception and taunting language. The devil was saying, and I am paraphrasing here, "If you are the Son of God like You claim to be, just do a miracle and feed yourself. It's that simple." But Jesus didn't act on the temptation. He simply said no and quoted from the book of Deuteronomy back to the enemy.

Temptation #2

Then the devil took him to the holy city, Jerusalem, to the highest point of the Temple, and said, "If you are the Son of God, jump off! For the Scriptures say,
'He will order his angels to protect you.
And they will hold you up with their hands
   so you won't even hurt your foot on a stone.'"
Jesus responded, "The Scriptures also say, 'You must not test the LORD your God.'" (Matthew 4:5–7)

Once again we hear the jab, "If you actually are the Son of God, make sure that Your father will protect You down here by flinging Yourself off this pinnacle." Essentially, Satan was saying that God would never let Jesus die. Yet, Jesus knew that the cross was coming down the road. Again, He responded with a quote from Deuteronomy.

Temptation #3

Next the devil took him to the peak of a very high mountain and showed him all the kingdoms of the world and their glory. "I will give it all to you," he said, "if you will kneel down and worship me."

"Get out of here, Satan," Jesus told him. "For the Scriptures say,

'You must worship the Lord your God
and serve only him.'" (Matthew 4:8–10)

Again, the devil took Jesus up to a high point and finally stopped with the identity tactics. This time, he went straight for his end goal by saying, "Worship me, and I'll give you this world." Ironically, the enemy has no authority to give anything of the world to anyone. But, that's certainly what he tried to do with Jesus here. This time, when Christ told the enemy to leave, he had to obey His authority.

Next, we find two interesting sentences. First, verse 11: "Then the devil went away, and angels came and took care of Jesus." Second, in most Bibles we find a heading that reads something like "The Ministry of Jesus Begins." Some Bibles may offer different wording, but the meaning is the same. The misery in the wilderness was over, and His mission began.

Just like we talked about yesterday, Jesus showed His faithfulness toward God in every single test as a testimony for us. We can live out our calling to our mission because we walk alongside a Savior who has felt hunger, humility, thirst, pain, loneliness, and exhaustion and who showed us how to say no to temptations. In the midst of His misery, He was offered the riches and glory of this world and refused it all, so we can too. Walking in freedom means to keep serving Jesus, even when things get hard. Sometimes, really hard.

When we begin the mission that God has called us to, we will also experience questions from Satan to tempt us and get us to stop what we do for the Lord, just as he did with Jesus.

- **Temptation #1**—Is God really going to *provide* for You if You do His work?
- **Temptation #2**—Is God really going to *protect* You if You do His work?
- **Temptation #3**—Is God really going to give You His *power* to do His work?

When I told you earlier about being stuck in California with just twenty dollars for three days when my family only had eighty-seven cents left, here's the other side of that story: that same day, my record label and management team called to tell me that my first single on Christian radio had broken into the top twenty. Even in such miserable circumstances, God was showing my family and me that He was blessing the mission He called us to. He was providing. He was protecting. He was showing us His power.

That same power is available for your journey, whether you're in the midst of personal misery or experiencing an incredible season in your own mission.

Next-Step Questions

Have any fears or concerns about the kind of misery we have talked about today kept you from God's mission for you?

_____

_____

With your specific skills, talents, and gifts, what mission do you believe God has called you to? Explain.

_____

_____

Considering your personal mission, what is your one step of faith to take today?

_____

_____

> In our *MISSION*,
> some days will be messy,
> some mysterious,
> and some *MAJESTIC*.

21

Retracing Your Steps

A s we are now very close to the midpoint of our journey, taking one step at a time, we're going to go to a very practical place today. Our victim mindset, our crippled and conflicted state, our earthly struggles and tests, along with all the daily misery we experience, can cause us to feel discounted and beat down. We may doubt our ability to be a part of accomplishing God's purposes. Even if you've made it this far in the book, there are likely still things that cause you to say, "God cannot possibly use *that*. Why would He want to use my [*fill in the blank*]?"

Well, here's the good news. That is not up to you. What God decides to use is up to Him. That's why He's God and we're not: "But God showed his great love for us by sending Christ to die for us while we were still sinners" (Romans 5:8).

When did God show His great love? When did Christ die? After we got our act together? When we finally worked hard enough to convince Him we were righteous? No! "While we were still sinners." (This verse is repeated from Step 1 for emphasis here.)

Today—not tomorrow or down the road when you feel like you're ready—who needs to hear your story? Who needs your help? Have you experienced a loss, an addiction, a disease, or some other human struggle, and God has someone right now whom He wants you to help? Whatever you have already walked through, or are walking through now, you went through it for a purpose, for someone else's good. Because nothing is wasted with God.

For this week's retracing step, we're going to add an exercise with your review. I want to encourage you, for your own growth and maturity, to take the time to do both. Before your review of the past six steps, here's an exercise that can change someone's life and affect your own in ways you might never have thought possible.

Your Testimony

A very simple way to share your story of how Christ has changed your life is to write out your testimony by completing these open-ended statements in two to four sentences each. Once you've written it out, you can then read through it several times to see how you can easily share this with someone in just a few minutes.

My life before Christ . . .

_____

_____

_____

I came to know Jesus through/because of . . .

_____

_____

_____

My relationship with Jesus has changed my life by . . .

_____

_____

_____

Today, God is working in my life by/through . . .

_____

_____

_____

Retracing Your Steps Questions

What was the easiest step for you to take this week?

_____

_____

What was the hardest step you took this week?

_____

_____

Name *all* the steps of faith you chose to take this week.

_____

_____

What can you carry out of this week into the rest of your life?

_____

_____

Carry to Cast

We've all heard the phrase, "Yeah, he has a lot of baggage" or, "She's never going to get over that if she doesn't get rid of some baggage." We know the context means there is something painful, hurtful, and damaging that happened in the past and the person is carrying that hurt into the present, every day. Whatever occurred could be the fault of the person, but sometimes it's not their fault at all.

Remember the last time you had to carry something heavy for a good distance? Depending on how far you had to go, even something that felt light at first could become really difficult to carry. So, what's the deal? Did the thing actually get heavier with each step? Of course not. It didn't gain weight, but with each step, your energy was expended and your strength decreased. The farther you walked, the heavier the weight *felt*.

The same is true with emotional and spiritual baggage. The longer we carry around toxic issues in our hearts like unforgiveness, bitterness, jealousy, and hatred, the harder it gets and the heavier the weight feels.

I shared a verse earlier—1 Peter 5:7—that, over time, has become a favorite of every generation. Take a look at these four different Bible versions.

> Give all your worries and cares to God, for he cares about you. (NLT)
> Cast all your anxiety on him because he cares for you. (NIV)
> Leave all your worries with him, because he cares for you. (GNT)
> God cares for you, so turn all your worries over to him. (CEV)

Regardless of the wording, Peter encouraged Christ's followers to carry no baggage—to stop walking and hand it over to God. Leave it with Him along with all your worries. To walk in freedom means not to carry the weight of the world that we were never designed to hold in the first place. The language here actually means to *throw* our cares to God. Get rid of them quickly. He knows what to do with them all. On the other hand, if we choose to keep carrying the weight, we will eventually lose strength, stumble, and fall.

We tend to think of 1 Peter 5:7 as encouraging us to only give God the hard things, the bad stuff that we go through in life. But, as sinners, we have to be careful even with the good things. We shouldn't just apply this truth to something negative. Sometimes the best things can hold us back from running our race. Look at Hebrews 12:1.

Therefore, since we are surrounded by such a huge crowd of witnesses to the life of faith, let us strip off every weight that slows us down, especially the sin that so easily trips us up. And let us run with endurance the race God has set before us.

The author used the phrase "every weight," and then added "especially the sin." So a "weight" could be anything that becomes hard for us to carry. The language refers to *anything* that hinders us in the race God marked out for us. Because of our sin nature, we can take something good, any blessing in our lives, and make it unhealthy or even toxic. For example, ministering to people, which is supposed to be one of our primary roles as Christ-followers, can be placed above family or before God. We can even make a ministry about us and create an idol. This makes total sense when we read Jesus's warning in Matthew 7:21–23, a passage we used from The Message Bible in Step 17 under a different context:

> Not everyone who calls out to me, "Lord! Lord!" will enter the Kingdom of Heaven. Only those who actually do the will of my Father in heaven will enter. On judgment day many will say to me, "Lord! Lord! We prophesied in your name and cast out demons in your name and performed many miracles in your name." But I will reply, "I never knew you. Get away from me, you who break God's laws."

Now, let's move on in Hebrews 12 to verses 2-3:

> We do this by keeping our eyes on Jesus, the champion who initiates and perfects our faith. Because of the joy awaiting him, he endured the cross,

disregarding its shame. Now he is seated in the place of honor beside God's throne. Think of all the hostility he endured from sinful people; then you won't become weary and give up.

Because sin wants our hearts to belong to the wrong things, we can so easily lose sight of the *right* things. In taking steps of faith, we have to constantly be honest with ourselves to ask if we need to set aside anything we are carrying: success, social status, or personal agenda. Sometimes, we will even have to take a hard look at our hopes and dreams. Sacrificing any of these places in our hearts and lives is going to be tough. But, sometimes, it's exactly what we need to do.

With this being such a big step, here are some questions to consider:

- If I decided to stop carrying this weight, could I take a *bigger* step of faith?
- If I decided to stop carrying this weight, could I take a *bolder* step of faith?
- If I decided to stop carrying this weight, what could I accomplish that I never could before?
- Am I holding on to anything that I shouldn't be?

This step is about constantly taking inventory of what we are carrying and being aware if we need to cast it onto God. One of the many reasons that He called us sheep was because they are not beasts of burden. They can carry nothing. In Matthew 11:28, Jesus said, "Come to me, all of you who are weary and carry heavy burdens, and I will give you rest." Always remember, for every step on your path, Jesus offers to carry you.

Next-Step Questions

What is the biggest weight—a bad or good thing—you are carrying today? Why do you keep holding on?

_____

_____

Take a few minutes to write down any of your thoughts on the questions I previously asked you. Here they are again:

- If I decided to stop carrying this weight, could I take a *bigger* step of faith?
- If I decided to stop carrying this weight, could I take a *bolder* step of faith?
- If I decided to stop carrying this weight, what could I accomplish that I never could before?
- Am I holding on to anything that I shouldn't be?

_____

_____

_____

_____

Casting off to God needless weight you're carrying, what is your one step of faith to take today?

_____

_____

When we **START** to carry worry, it's time to cast off the **WEIGHT**.

STEP

23

Safety to Sacrifice

Safety is a high priority today. Homes have security systems. Cars have all sorts of safety features. Phones have passcodes. Web accounts have usernames and passwords. We buy all kinds of insurance for financial protection, including our identities. From the physical world to the digital realm, we value a sense of safety. Whether we are actually safe or not, we will go to great lengths and expense to feel secure.

Compare that to the fear we have any time someone mentions the word *sacrifice*. We cringe because we view that as loss, not gain. Culturally, we no longer view sacrifice as an honor, but as an intrusion, an interruption. Yes, sacrifice will take us out of our safety zone and force us into the open. We must come to a place of seeing sacrifice not just as a hard choice for today, but, rather, an investment in the future. We don't take the long view. Instead, we say things like, "I'm just not sure I can sacrifice that much time and energy right now" or, "I'm not ready for that kind of sacrifice." We tend to use the word when we feel we will lose more than we might gain.

But sacrifice shouldn't really be about us or our sense of safety, but rather about being truly focused on what others need.

While modern cultural concepts constantly change, biblical meanings stand firm and are unchanging. The word *sacrifice* has always meant the same thing in Scripture, and Jesus forever changed everything as the Lamb who was slain. When we follow Him, the sacrifice of sin has been paid, but the sacrifice of self must occur daily. Romans 12:1 is a well-known verse.

> And so, dear brothers and sisters, I plead with you to give your bodies to God because of all he has done for you. Let them be a living and holy sacrifice—the kind he will find acceptable. This is truly the way to worship him.

In Paul's statement, he connected being a sacrifice to life, not death; to holiness, not payment for sin; to being close to God, not pulling away; to worship of Him, not of ourselves. Those are all good things. Wins, not losses. But, let's take a look at how we can still get this concept wrong.

We sacrifice on the wrong altar.

We can do things that are *good* but that aren't necessarily *God*. We can get our priorities completely mixed up. Remember the verses yesterday in which Jesus listened to the people talk about all the ministry they had done and then He said He didn't know them? All those sacrifices were on an altar, just not *His* altar. Well-meaning people, in the name of

God, do all kinds of things that have nothing to do with Him. Sacrificing on the wrong altar can feel like a safe thing, the right thing, but it can be very dangerous eternally.

We sacrifice the wrong thing.

We can often lay someone or something on the altar that was never intended to be placed there. The Pharisees and Sadducees were always at the temple, giving of their time, energy, and attention, but they wouldn't sacrifice their egos, agendas, positions, and titles—the very thing Jesus kept trying to get them to hand over so they could finally see who He was. Instead, they sacrificed many good things like generosity, purity, kindness, and compassion to place themselves over the very people they should have been helping:

> Then the Lord said to him, "You Pharisees are so careful to clean the outside of the cup and the dish, but inside you are filthy—full of greed and wickedness! Fools! Didn't God make the inside as well as the outside? (Luke 11:39–40)

We keep crawling off the altar when the time comes to die to self.

As sinners, putting God and others before ourselves is not our first choice. Any time we sense we are being told to take a backseat and give up our "rights," we will choose our own safety every time. That usually means the last place we go will be the altar where we sacrifice our own ego. We decide that giving is having to lose something valuable. We decide that helping someone is a hassle, a waste of our time and energy. We place our focus on material things, social status, and how the world views us.

So, how do we not choose our own false sense of safety and instead stay on God's altar? Well, we must change what we value and what we think. This brings us to Romans 12:2:

> Don't copy the behavior and customs of this world, but let God transform you into a new person by changing the way you think. Then you will learn to know God's will for you, which is good and pleasing and perfect.

According to today's verses, only one thing is to be sacrificed voluntarily on our altar: ourselves. No one else. Nothing else. Just us. We truly walk in freedom when we crawl up on the altar and offer ourselves before God, to die to self and to live for Him. Ironically, our need for feeling safe often unknowingly traps us in a room with something that will hurt us. When Christ calls us to follow Him, He also offers the foundational promises of God for that walk of faith. While this may feel like a massive sacrifice, we are walking into authentic security under His protection, where any sacrificial step we take will lead to ultimate safety.

Next-Step Questions

Why do you suppose so many things in this world that we consider to be safe are not safe at all?

_____

_____

What are some ways you need to transform your thinking to hand over your own ego and agenda to God?

_____

_____

In moving further out of your comfort zone, what is your one step of faith to take today?

_____

_____

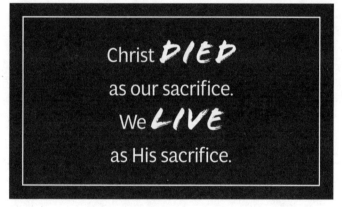

Christ *DIED*
as our sacrifice.
We *LIVE*
as His sacrifice.

24

Reckless to Relentless

A few years ago I was on a tour for which Zane Black was the speaker. Part of his role was to lead all the artists in "tour church," a time when everyone gathered together for worship and a message. One Sunday morning, Zane gave a sermon on Jesus's parable of the sower and the seed. That teaching has stuck with me ever since. Here's the passage in Matthew 13:3–9.

> Then he told them many things in parables, saying: "A farmer went out to sow his seed. As he was scattering the seed, some fell along the path, and the birds came and ate it up. Some fell on rocky places, where it did not have much soil. It sprang up quickly, because the soil was shallow. But when the sun came up, the plants were scorched, and they withered because they had no root. Other seed fell among thorns, which grew up and choked the plants.

Still other seed fell on good soil, where it produced
a crop—a hundred, sixty or thirty times what was
sown. Whoever has ears, let them hear." (NIV)

So, this farmer (or sower in some versions) is throwing the seed onto all different types of ground. Whatever he threw into the good soil produced a lot. But the other, not so much. The seed he threw onto the rocky ground went in but didn't take because the roots couldn't go deep enough to survive and grow. The seed that went into the thorns also took, but then the thorns wrapped around and killed it. The seed he threw near the walking path never took because, essentially, it became birdseed.

Up until Zane's teaching on this parable, I had heard this sermon many times. I had read this chapter countless times on my own. Always before, the focus had been on the seed. When you read or hear this story, it's actually really easy to forget about the person throwing the seed, because you keep hearing about what happened to the seed itself. The application for me has always been focused on protecting the seed and how we need to find "good ground."

But, here was the difference in Zane's teaching: God can still grow good things in hard places.

Bottom line is that Jesus was and is the Farmer, the Sower. He went into Samaria, a region with a reputation for not being "good ground." He was constantly in the face of the Pharisees, men with hard-as-a-rock hearts and thorny souls. Jesus walked into so many situations and places off the beaten path where a rabbi would never have gone, encountering demons and the dead. He stood on hillside after hillside sowing into the hardest ground of that day.

So, was Jesus being reckless with God's seed, the message of the Kingdom? Was He just casting it out freely anywhere without a plan or thought?

No, He was not at all reckless. He was relentless.

Now, let's be honest. Some semantics are involved with these two words. Dictionary.com offers this definition for reckless: "utterly unconcerned about the consequences of some action; without caution; careless." *Relentless* is "not easing or slacking; maintaining speed, vigor."

Many watched Jesus's ministry and called Him reckless. The Pharisees were a consistent example. They questioned Jesus's actions at every turn, as in Mark 2:16: "But when the teachers of religious law who were Pharisees saw him eating with tax collectors and other sinners, they asked his disciples, "Why does he eat with such scum?" In fact, they finally decided He was so reckless that He had to die.

But, Jesus was relentless. His declaration of the gospel was fully focused on the redemption of sin. In His teaching, He continued to caution and show care to everyone He encountered. Between His baptism and His ascension, He never eased up on His ministry. Yes, Christ went off alone to pray. He pulled away from the crowds with His disciples to rest. But then He went right back into the midst of humanity, sowing the seed of the Kingdom.

The lesson I learned that Sunday morning and that I'm passing on to you today is that we cannot give up when the conditions don't look perfect or when we don't find what we might deem to be "good ground." We have to believe in the gospel so much that we will cast anywhere and everywhere, because we never know what God might do and what He might use to reach someone. Even in a very hard place.

We have to be farmers, walking down the highway, throwing seed, just wanting to see something take root and grow. We have to be relentless.

One of the observations of the twenty-first-century church in our culture is that we focus far too much on protecting the seed. We have wanted to choose where it goes and who gets it. But, we don't get to decide who is beyond salvation or past redemption. *That* attitude is reckless. The truth is, in every generation, the gospel always stands on its own and does not and will not return void, as Isaiah 55:11 states:

> I send it out, and it always produces fruit.
> It will accomplish all I want it to,
>> and it will prosper everywhere I send it.

We must believe that God can plant something amazing in the craziest of conditions to overcome the toughest expectations. Walking in the freedom of Christ will mean we take steps into hard places where there is drought, rocks, and thorns—the real places where the gospel is needed and will thrive. We simply cast the seed and trust God with where it goes and who it grows in. When we are talking to someone and we sense God nudging us to share Him, it can be so easy to think, *Oh, God, they don't want to hear that right now. I'm not casting it here.* But, the sower doesn't get to decide who deserves the seed. That's being reckless, not relentless.

The gospel is about believing that everyone deserves the opportunity to experience forgiveness and the transformation that only Jesus can bring. As you walk forward today, watch for the places that God would want you to cast His seed for the sake of others. One of the most exciting blessings for the Christ-follower is to be a part of the spread of the gospel.

Next-Step Questions

What are some of the things that stop you from sharing your faith? Explain.

_____

_____

Who in your life needs you to be relentless with the gospel, faithfully offering the good seed, no matter the soil?

_____

_____

Choosing to be relentless with the gospel, what is your one step of faith to take today?

_____

_____

The difference between reckless and relentless is *REASON* and *RESOLVE*.

———————————

Useless to Useful

To connect to yesterday, if we are reckless with the seeds of the gospel, we become useless to the work of the Kingdom. When we agree to be relentless with sharing what God has done in our lives, that obedience makes us useful while also giving us purpose, satisfaction, and contentment as we live out what He has called us to do.

What if the sower decided to save up all his seed for just the right time? What if he got to the end of his life with a lot of unsown seed? Today, we'll look at another parable from Jesus, one where He pointed out what God feels is useless and useful.

The Kingdom of Heaven can be illustrated by the story of a man going on a long trip. He called together his servants and entrusted his money to them while he was gone. He gave five bags of silver to one, two bags of silver to another, and one bag of silver to the last—dividing it in proportion to their abilities. He then left on his trip. (Matthew 25:14–15)

Think about how many of your friends you would hand over your money to. It is clear in the last sentence that the man divided his money based on what he believed each servant could handle. With your friends, to whom would you give a thousand dollars to watch over for you? To whom would you entrust a hundred? Are there some friends you'd only give maybe a ten?

Those questions put relationships in perspective as far as trust, responsibility, and confidence. Let's see how things panned out in our parable:

The servant who received the five bags of silver began to invest the money and earned five more. The servant with two bags of silver also went to work and earned two more. But the servant who received the one bag of silver dug a hole in the ground and hid the master's money. (Matthew 25:16–18)

Every investment involves some level of risk. When financial planners begin a relationship with a new client, one of the key factors to find out in the initial interview is the person's risk tolerance. Are they very conservative? Will they stay up all night worrying about their return? Or do they understand that the higher the risk, the more potential for a strong return? Maybe the answer is somewhere in the middle with a diverse mix. Trusting someone with our finances will always be a huge deal, especially when everything is dependent on that person making the right calls on the best investment for the optimal return.

With that information in mind, what if six months after the interview, the client contacted the planner only to be told, "Yeah, I could tell you couldn't handle any risk, so I dug a hole and buried it all. But the good news is I know exactly where your money is! Every single dollar!"? Would that be useless? Of course, because the client could have done that without anyone's help.

So what did the master do when he returned to find what his servants had done with his money?

> After a long time their master returned from his trip and called them to give an account of how they had used his money. The servant to whom he had entrusted the five bags of silver came forward with five more and said, "Master, you gave me five bags of silver to invest, and I have earned five more." . . . The servant who had received the two bags of silver came forward and said, "Master, you gave me two bags of silver to invest, and I have earned two more." (Matthew 25:19–20, 22)

In verses 21 and 23, we read an identical response to each: The master said, "Well done, my good and faithful servant. You have been faithful in handling this small amount, so now I will give you many more responsibilities. Let's celebrate together!"

Next up is our one-bag man who hid the money. (Fair warning—this is not pretty.)

> Master, I knew you were a harsh man, harvesting crops you didn't plant and gathering crops you didn't cultivate. I was afraid I would lose your money, so I

hid it in the earth. Look, here is your money back.
(Matthew 25:24–25)

Do you see the key phrase in the man's answer? "I was afraid." And then we read, "so I hid." Where have we read that before? Genesis 3 with Adam and Eve when they realized they had sinned. The bottom line is living a life full of fear is useless and can keep us from being useful. This kind of fear can cause us to not sow the seed and not invest because we are so scared of any risk. For the one-bag man, there were serious consequences for the choice and also a loss of blessing and reward. No risk, no reward.

> But the master replied, "You wicked and lazy servant! If you knew I harvested crops I didn't plant and gathered crops I didn't cultivate, why didn't you deposit my money in the bank? At least I could have gotten some interest on it."
> Then he ordered, "Take the money from this servant, and give it to the one with the ten bags of silver. To those who use well what they are given, even more will be given, and they will have an abundance. But from those who do nothing, even what little they have will be taken away." (Matthew 25:26–29)

One of the major points of this parable is to show us the massive difference in God's perspective and that of sinners. Total opposites. While the level of risk in being useful to the master was totally up to the person, taking zero risk, doing nothing, even avoiding common sense weren't acceptable at all. The point was investing whatever was given and then giving back *more*. Not hiding out of fear, but taking action in faith. Walking in freedom.

What good is anything God gives us when we hide or bury it when the goal is to be put to use? What good are the gifts of God if we don't share them with others? God gives us all of Himself upon salvation. From there, the level to which we are obedient, to which we will risk, invest, and sow is left up to us. But, anything we give to Him is then multiplied through the power of the Holy Spirit to allow us to experience what being useful to the Kingdom can truly mean.

Next-Step Questions

Why do you suppose the enemy would want us to always feel useless to God and even to others?

_____

_____

What are your "bags of silver" that God has handed over to you? How can you invest even more to grow everything He has given you?

_____

_____

In being certain you are useful in the Kingdom, what is your one step of faith to take today?

_____

_____

The greater the obedience,
the greater the risk.
The greater the *RISK*,
the greater the *REWARD*.

Roaming to Rooted

The phrase, "Not all who wander are lost" is a nice sentiment. The words can look great on a framed print or even a tattoo. But those kinds of cultural ideas tend to offer people an excuse from living a life of purpose in the now. What if someone told you, "I'm just wandering through life, but I'm not lost." Sounds kind of contradictory, right? Well, we all know that regardless of our age or stage in life, we can have seasons when we struggle with our purpose. We feel like we're randomly roaming when we just want to be rooted.

Today, in our next step, let's take a look at some of God's Word that offers us real roots in this life and can keep us safe from roaming without purpose.

His Promises

Many theologians have attempted to count the number of promises God made to us in His Word. While the amount varies by interpretation, the range is approximately 7,500 to 9,500. So, let's just say that there are thousands of promises for us. Jeremiah 29:11 is one of the most popular. The words are most often used as a reassurance that no matter how things might look at the time, God is always at work in the lives of His followers: "'For I know the plans I have for you,' declares the LORD, 'plans to prosper you and not to harm you, plans to give you hope and a future'" (NIV).

That verse is taken from the prophet Jeremiah's letter on behalf of God to the leaders of Israel. It was read to the people whom King Nebuchadnezzar had exiled from Jerusalem to Babylon. The words were to be shared to show how God would fulfill His promises to those who had been exiled and were forced into roaming, pulled up from the roots of their homeland. (Daniel was included in that group of people.)

God's thousands of promises show us His plan and create roots for who we are in Him. His promises keep us from roaming, from wandering lost.

His Protection

Jesus told us many times how our obedience doesn't guarantee we won't have trouble, but God as our Father will secure and anchor us in Him when the storms come. (Here, we are intentionally repeating Jesus's teaching about the wise builder from Step 17 to drive this point home.)

> I will show you what it's like when someone comes to me, listens to my teaching, and then follows it. It is like a person building a house who digs deep and lays the foundation on solid rock. When the

floodwaters rise and break against that house, it stands firm because it is well built. But anyone who hears and doesn't obey is like a person who builds a house right on the ground, without a foundation. When the floods sweep down against that house, it will collapse into a heap of ruins. (Luke 6:47–49)

A foundation is essentially the roots of a house. No one just starts building their walls on the ground. Jesus said that those who listen to and obey Him "dig deep." In terrains where the ground moves a lot, builders will pour what are called "piers," concrete columns that go down deep into the ground, much like the poles that go in to the ground below the water at a marina. The house will actually sit on the concrete piers so that no matter how much the surface ground moves, the house is secured on the supports that are buried in the earth. That is the picture of what Jesus offers us when we listen, trust, and obey His words. He protects us in the foundation or roots He provides.

His Productivity

Inside His promises and protection, His roots allow us to produce fruit from our lives that we could never grow on our own. In John 15, which we first mentioned in Step 10, Jesus gave us a great analogy for how He accomplishes His designed purposes in our lives:

I am the true grapevine, and my Father is the gardener. He cuts off every branch of mine that doesn't produce fruit, and he prunes the branches that do bear fruit so they will produce even more. You have already been pruned and purified by the message I have given you. Remain in me, and I will remain in you. For a branch cannot produce fruit if it is severed from the vine, and you cannot be fruitful unless you remain in me.

Yes, I am the vine; you are the branches. Those who remain in me, and I in them, will produce much fruit. For apart from me you can do nothing. . . . When you produce much fruit, you are my true disciples. This brings great glory to my Father. (John 15:1–5, 8)

Jesus was quite clear here. In Him, lots of fruit. Outside of Him, nothing. This goes back to our useless-and-useful step. Bad fruit is useless to everyone. God's fruit is a blessing to anyone who experiences it. Once we see fruit and how it blesses people, we no longer focus on the roots. We don't have to be concerned with roaming without a purpose. We simply *be* in Him, remain on the vine, and abide in Him, and the fruit will come.

His Provision

God will not only provide what we need, but as we stay rooted in Him, His fruit in our lives provides for others: "The Holy Spirit produces this kind of fruit in our lives: love, joy, peace, patience, kindness, goodness, faithfulness, gentleness, and self-control" (Galatians 5:22–23).

A tree never eats its own fruit. Its nourishment comes from its roots. The fruit is just the tree fulfilling its identity, its purpose. Through our roots, our fruit can help those around us who are roaming and looking for answers. They can be drawn to God's love, joy, peace, and so on, which He has produced in us for their benefit and His glory.

His Prosperity

In some Christian circles, prosperity is equated only with material wealth. But God has never defined anything of Him through the standards of this world. There's nothing wrong or sinful about wealth, but it should never be the focus of the Christian life as an expectation or standard. The prosperity and blessing from God that is most important and that we should seek is to become deeply rooted in Him. There we find strength, thankfulness, and increasing faith, which is true prosperity—those things that money can't buy.

> Then Christ will make his home in your hearts as you trust in him. Your roots will grow down into God's love and keep you strong. (Ephesians 3:17)

> Let your roots grow down into him, and let your lives be built on him. Then your faith will grow strong in the truth you were taught, and you will overflow with thankfulness. (Colossians 2:7)

Let's close this step by going back to Jesus's promise that our house can weather any storm if it is built on Him. Notice He did not say that our house has to be immaculate or beautiful or bigger than anyone else's. Our home simply must be built on and rooted in His promises for us to help us get to wherever we are walking on this journey.

Next-Step Questions

What causes you to roam, for your heart to wander? Be specific.

_____

_____

Which of the five "P" words and Scriptures spoke to you today? Explain.

_____

_____

In becoming more rooted in Christ, what is your one step of faith to take today?

_____

_____

God **PROMISES** to
protect, provide, produce,
and prosper
us in His **WAYS** and
His **WILL**.

People-Pleaser to Peacemaker

When someone uses the term *people-pleaser* today, we know that the connotation is a person who will do just about anything to make sure everyone is happy with him or her. Pleasing someone we care about is a good thing, but working overtime to make sure we are approved of at all times is exhausting. The more a people-pleaser struggles to keep everyone happy, the more tired he or she becomes. The most common characteristics are avoiding conflict at all costs, saying whatever will deflect attention from addressing the real problem, and being patronizing when necessary.

On the other hand, when we decide to become a peacemaker in any situation, the end goal is resolution and reconciliation. But until then, a lot of work is typically required to get there. Back in Step 18, we talked about the Beatitudes, or the Sermon on the Mount. For today's step, we'll start by revisiting

Jesus's words in Matthew 5:9: "God blesses those who work for peace, for they will be called the children of God."

First, notice the words *work for peace*. We live in a culture that has become increasingly violent, yet ironically, on the other end of the spectrum, also very much into appeasing everyone to avoid conflict. The Internet and social media have allowed anyone to have a voice into almost everyone's life, all anonymously. Reading everything from reviews to comments to threads quickly reveals how hateful we have become as a people. Disagreement is no longer civil but instead filled with fighting words. So, Jesus said (and I'm paraphrasing), "You want to see who *My* kids are? Look for those who work to bring My peace into this world."

God never called us as His followers to just *keep* the peace. We are called to *make* peace—make, as in create, usher in, cause, and construct peace where peace has ceased or where there was none before.

Let's look at three areas of life where God wants us to experience His peace:

Area #1: In Our Hearts

Therefore, since we have been made right in God's sight by faith, we have peace with God because of what Jesus Christ our Lord has done for us. (Romans 5:1)

We cannot offer something we don't have ourselves. We can't give away something we have never experienced. The only way to encounter authentic personal peace is to have peace with God through a relationship with Christ. Once that heart connection has been made, we can daily connect to and grow in that peace. Going back to what we talked about yesterday, the fruit of peace can grow out of the vine into which we are rooted.

> Don't worry about anything; instead, pray about everything. Tell God what you need, and thank him for all he has done. Then you will experience God's peace, which exceeds anything we can understand. His peace will guard your hearts and minds as you live in Christ Jesus. (Philippians 4:6–7)

God's peace is not of this world. It is beyond what we can naturally understand and comprehend. The experience of His peace actually creates a protection around our hearts and minds, freeing us from fear, anxiety, and worry, even in the face of a crisis. Prayer calls on peace to come and rule our hearts and minds.

We can only bring true peace to *any* situation as an overflow from our relationship with Christ. Being a peacemaker will always begin by making sure our own hearts are at peace.

Area # 2: In Our Circles

When our hearts are at peace through Christ, that peace will begin to overflow to those we love and care about. As selfish sinners—especially inside our families, where we live so closely together—when a relational fire starts, we can bring a gas can and make things worse. Out of hurt and pain, we can push peace away, believing we are protecting ourselves. But just one person who is pursuing Christ's peace can change the dynamic in a family by bringing water to put out the fire.

In most twelve-step addiction recovery programs, step 8 has to do with attempting to make peace with anyone who has been hurt. Step 9 is the proactive step in that process: "Make direct amends to such people wherever possible, except when to do so would injure them or others." Paul talked about the peace-making process in our relationships in Romans 12:18: "If it is possible, as far as it depends on you, live at peace with everyone" (NIV).

Notice the qualifiers Paul placed in this command. First, "if [peace] is possible." Next, "as far as [peace] depends on you." We cannot force peace on anyone. We cannot demand peace. That never works. At times and for any number of reasons, people just aren't ready for reconciliation, forgiveness, or redemption. In those circumstances, we are only called to display peace, keep the peace, and constantly make it known that peace is available.

Area #3: In Our World

God does not give us peace just so we can experience it, but also so that we can go out and proactively make peace. As hate-filled as our culture has become, displaying God's peace through our lives is actually easier and sticks out today more than ever. When we see opportunities to help people, bring solutions to situations, and make something right that has been wrong, that is bringing the peace of God to earth. In every circumstance, He has a plan for how peace can be delivered by someone willing to work at it with Him.

> For God in all his fullness
> was pleased to live in Christ,

and through him God reconciled
>   everything to himself.
He made peace with everything in heaven and on
earth
>   by means of Christ's blood on the cross.
>   (Colossians 1:19–20)

Working to constantly please people is an exhausting and endless work. Choosing to please God may not make everyone happy, but it will certainly change the world—our own, that of those we love, and anyone we can reach in Jesus's name.

Next-Step Questions

Why do you think approval and acceptance from others is so important to most of us?

_____

_____

What is one place in your life where you can *keep* the peace? What is one place in your life where you need to *make* peace?

_____

_____

In giving up people-pleasing and bringing God's peace to others, what is your one step of faith to take today?

_____

_____

The more *PEACE* you give,
the more you *GET*.

28

Retracing Your Steps

As we go further into our steps and deeper into this journey, I know it's easy to get overwhelmed by thinking
about what needs to change, what you need to start doing,
what you need to stop doing, and anything you sense God
has convicted you to work on. With that in mind, let me
pause here and encourage you.

Any time we end up with twenty things on our list of
what we need to change, know that Satan gave it to us, not
God. Satan's goal is to make us feel overwhelmed so that we
end up changing nothing. Conversely, as a loving Father,
God is going to tell us one thing at a time that He wants us
to work on. So, we have to constantly be looking out for and
watching for our one thing.

Going through this book is intentionally placing you in a
position of hearing God and responding to His prompting on
various issues and concerns. Each step can help you discover

your one thing right now—to find the big picture of what God wants to accomplish in you today.

Are you or have you become too distracted and over-whelmed by twenty things with which Satan keeps hammer-ing you? Remember, the only way to peel an onion is one layer at a time, so we should allow God to do the same thing with our issues in life.

Check out how the New Century Bible gives us Philippians 3:13–14:

> Brothers and sisters, I know that I have not yet reached that goal, but there is one thing I always do. Forgetting the past and straining toward what is ahead, I keep trying to reach the goal and get the prize for which God called me through Christ to the life above.

Keeping the "one thing, not twenty" in mind as you review Steps 22 through 27, take a look at how you are going to step toward the following:

- casting all your cares on Jesus
- committing daily to life on the altar and transform-ing into the image of Christ
- being relentless with the gospel and God's message of reconciliation
- committing to obedience in being useful to God's purposes and plan
- growing ever-deepening roots from the Vine
- the art of peace-making in every place where God allows you to walk

Retracing Your Steps Questions

What was the easiest step for you to take this week?

_____

_____

What was the hardest step you took this week?

_____

_____

Name *all* the steps of faith you chose to take this week.

_____

_____

What can you carry out of this week into the rest of your life?

_____

_____

29

Rules to Relationship

Our oldest son, Noah (sixteen at the time of this writing), is a classic firstborn. All his life, he has been our resident rule-follower. One time, when he was around four years old, our family went to visit some friends for the first time. After we pulled into their driveway and I stopped the car, Noah announced to everyone, "OK, I've never been here before. Please tell me all the rules so I don't do anything wrong."

That characteristic has always been a part of Noah's DNA. Now learning to drive, he wants to understand all the rules of the road before he gets behind the wheel of a car. Or when he's away from home with friends, he'll text us to ask about doing something *before* he does it. Our son definitely covers all the bases. He measures twice and cuts once, as they say.

The advantage for a parent when a child thinks like this is obvious: you're far more likely to have a well-behaved son or daughter. The downside is you don't want your child to live in fear, focus on punishment, or only worry about the rules. Because of this dynamic, for Noah, we've had to work on teaching him about grace.

For far too many people, a relationship with Jesus becomes more about trying to not mess up than focusing on the freedom and abundant life He offers. The rules are always placed before the relationship because they believe the relationship is only about the rules. An analogy to living life this way is like being in a jail cell and someone coming to unlock the door, but we refuse to open it, step out, and walk in freedom.

Trying to constantly avoid mistakes is no way to live. That only produces fear and guilt. To drive home that thought on our step today, I want to offer a different side of James 1:22, a popular verse: "But don't just listen to God's word. You must do what it says."

We often read these words only in the context of making sure we act on and apply God's Word. But there's more to this verse. God has not called us to be *don't-ers* of the Word, but *doers*. Our responsibility is to take everything He has given us and to see those things through and brought to fulfillment. The Ten Commandments were not given to us just so we could know we aren't good enough. They are to let us see our need for a Savior—One who has come to offer us His righteousness despite, and because of, our shortcomings. They are there to lead us toward a relationship with Him, to lead us toward a continually deeper level of holiness.

As Christ-followers, we aren't supposed to focus our lives on how well we can keep rules *or* how badly we can break them. Where we keep our eyes is on Jesus, the Author and

Perfector of our faith, the One who can transform us to look more and more like Him. Our need causes us to follow Him, which then allows us to abide with Him, like a branch to a vine as we've seen in John 15.

The Pharisees were dead set on trying to abide by the hundreds of rules they had added to the original Ten Commandments. They placed those demands on all the people as well. And so those rules burdened and overwhelmed everyone. In Matthew 5:17, Jesus said, "Do not think that I have come to abolish the Law or the Prophets; I have not come to abolish them but to fulfill them" (NIV). But God's rules, even the original one that Adam and Eve violated, were simply meant for our protection and provision. For every commandment, law, or rule He has given, a catalyst drives its meaning. Humans often make rules for the sake of rules, but that is not God's way. He has a plan and a purpose. For the people who heard Jesus teach this—especially those proud of themselves for keeping all the rules—He offered a game-changing paradigm with this teaching:

> You have heard that our ancestors were told, "You must not murder. If you commit murder, you are subject to judgment." But I say, if you are even angry with someone, you are subject to judgment! . . .
>
> You have heard the commandment that says, "You must not commit adultery." But I say, anyone who even looks at a woman with lust has already committed adultery with her in his heart. (Matthew 5:21–22, 27–28)

So, anger in the heart to the point of hatred is murder in the mind. To whom? To a perfect God. Imagining adultery or premarital sex in the mind is equal to committing the act. To whom? To a perfect God. Suddenly, from that moment on in history, everyone was now a lot more guilty per the explanation of how God views sin. Does acting on a thought make everything worse? Of course. But the sin occurs in the entertainment of and focus on the original temptation.

We've all heard people say that any sort of faith or need for a god or savior is just a crutch. For those folks, the idea of needing Jesus feels like a shortcoming. But the reality is, we are all crippled by the burden of sin; that's why we need Jesus if we are to walk in health and freedom. Our realization of our need for Christ leads us to a relationship with Him, as we answer His call to "Follow Me." There are going to be days when we fall short and break God's rules, but He also walks with us in forgiveness as the relationship grows stronger.

Next-Step Questions

How would you describe your relationship with rule-keeping? Do you tend to be a rule-follower or a rule-breaker? Explain.

_____

_____

How can a healthy understanding of God's love and grace draw us to Him and help us not focus so much on the dos and don'ts?

_____

_____

In focusing more on your relationship than on the rules, what is your one step of faith to take today?

_____

_____

> Focus on being a
> **DOER** of the Word,
> not a **DON'T-ER**

Selfish to Submissive

In 2 Kings 5, we find the story of Naaman and the prophet Elisha. As the head of the Syrian army, Naaman was a highly regarded military leader. The nation revered him as a war hero. The Bible referred to him as a "mighty warrior." But then tragedy struck his life. Something happened that he didn't see coming, and it changed everything. He was diagnosed with leprosy.

Not only was leprosy a death sentence that guaranteed a horribly slow and painful end, but he would now be considered ceremonially unclean. His life as a military leader was over. Naaman would no longer be able to lead anyone, much less an army. He would be forced to move to a leper colony to finish out what was left of his life.

But Naaman had one thing going for him: the king didn't want to lose his top general. Finding a soldier with that kind of track record for winning wars was not something the king wanted to have to do.

Ironically, a captive servant girl from Israel told Naaman's wife that a prophet named Elisha was in Samaria and could heal him if he would just go there. When Naaman heard this, he went to the king, who then granted him permission to go. But he also sent along an official letter requesting healing, as well as offering 750 pounds of silver, 150 pounds of gold, and ten sets of clothing for the king of Israel. This was a common practice, when one king requested some kind of favor or assistance from another king. The bigger the gift, the greater the chance of success.

When the king of Israel read the letter, he became angry and assumed it was some sort of trick. He knew only God—not any king—could heal. Yet when Elisha heard about what happened, he sent word to the king to send Naaman to him. As Naaman approached, Elisha offered an interesting command:

> Elisha sent a messenger out to him with this message: "Go and wash yourself seven times in the Jordan River. Then your skin will be restored, and you will be healed of your leprosy." (2 Kings 5:10)

Now, we have to remember that Naaman was a somebody, a celebrity, a war hero, a VIP leader with a big résumé and huge reputation. He was offended when only a messenger was sent out with some crazy instruction to go take a bath in a river. Bottom line: Naaman let his pride and ego get the best of him. In the moment, he forgot about his dire circumstances and reverted back to his previous life before leprosy. He even declared, "I expected him to wave his hand over the leprosy and call on the name of the LORD his God and heal me!" (v. 11) Naaman was obviously hoping for a big show or some sort of magical experience. And then, he also griped about the river. There were some far nicer and cleaner rivers back home, if that's all he needed to do.

But the officers with Naaman began to reason with him, saying how Elisha could have asked him to do something much more difficult than to go wash in a river. They asked him to reconsider. He agreed and finally chose to cooperate.

> So Naaman went down to the Jordan River and dipped himself seven times, as the man of God had instructed him. And his skin became as healthy as the skin of a young child, and he was healed! Then Naaman and his entire party went back to find the man of God. They stood before him, and Naaman said, "Now I know that there is no God in all the world except in Israel." (2 Kings 5:14–15)

For some reason, people in every generation want to associate the work of God with a big show. A production. An event that is so huge and supernatural it was, for sure, Him. We want writing in the sky. When it comes to our story, we want God to give us some big purpose that impresses everyone. So, we make choices like deciding that we won't talk to our neighbor for ten minutes, but we'll go to a foreign country on mission. We want to be placed on an important committee at church but won't volunteer to watch single moms' kids for an hour.

We pray for signs and miracles when God has already whispered an answer in the silence. Yet, most often, when we are expecting God to do something extravagant, something big, He just asks for a single step of obedience, away from our selfishness and pride. And because we're so busy being self-centered, we run the risk of missing out on what He offers. When Elisha promised healing through a simple step, Naaman's pride almost cost him his life. The same type of outcome can easily happen to us when we choose ourselves over submission to God.

When I started out in Christian music, many times I would go play my songs in front of ten kids who cared more about the pizza they were eating than what I was sharing from my heart. In those moments, it was so easy, so tempting, to imagine one day being on a big stage in an arena. It was easy to pray, "God, if you just put me up there in front of ten thousand people, I will be so faithful to your call."

But I finally discovered that God has to teach us and test us in front of the ten before He will trust us with the platform of thousands. Time after time, I had to submit myself and learn how to be obedient to giving Him my all when people weren't listening. I had to work really hard in tough circumstances to share the gospel. But in the midst of that, God was sharpening my skills and gifts, equipping me to one day walk into places that might look far cooler to many but were actually just big places with more broken people who need Him. With God, bigger is rarely better. He cares more about depth than width. And in the hard times, in the places where I may not have necessarily wanted to be, I was always inside the will of God.

Any day, any time, we can act like Naaman, thinking of ourselves as strong and mighty, but the reality is, we are falling apart. However, healing can come when we surrender our will and step into submission to the King.

Next-Step Questions

Where do you tend to struggle with pride, ego, and selfishness? Be specific.

_____

_____

Where is a small place in your life in which you can express big submission?

_____

_____

Replacing selfish desires with submission, what is your one step of faith to take today?

_____

_____

> Laying down our *PRIDE* allows us to *FIND* God's passion.

31

Superficial to Supernatural

In 1 Samuel 8, we are given an account that proves God will grant His children their request even when it is not His will. The proof of free will and of Him allowing us choices in His great love is clearly shown here. Basically, He says, this is not best, but if you think it's what you want, I will allow it. He grants permission that is not His provision.

The elders of Israel met with the prophet Samuel about rejecting his sons as their new leaders. Everyone knew they were not trustworthy and faithful like their father. But instead of asking Samuel to find out what God wanted, they came up with their own idea. The leaders had looked around at the other nations and thought having a king looked like a cool way to be governed. So, peer pressure got the best of them: "'Look,' they told him, 'you are now old, and your sons are not like you. Give us a king to judge us like all the other nations have'" (1 Samuel 8:5).

God's perspective on their request is very interesting and, of course, insightful. He saw this as a rejection, not of Samuel or his sons, but of Him. Did Israel not understand they already had the King of kings as their Leader?

> Samuel was displeased with their request and went to the LORD for guidance. "Do everything they say to you," the LORD replied, "for they are rejecting me, not you. They don't want me to be their king any longer. Ever since I brought them from Egypt they have continually abandoned me and followed other gods. And now they are giving you the same treatment. Do as they ask, but solemnly warn them about the way a king will reign over them." (1 Samuel 8:6–9)

Israel was a theocracy—a nation ruled by God. (An important side note here is that as His followers, regardless of whether we live geographically in a democracy or monarchy, we are spiritually citizens of a theocracy.) But they were now demanding to become a monarchy—ruled by, in this case, a man who would lead them.

Now remember, Samuel was a prophet, so he began to deliver a stern warning from God about their choice. Basically, he told them (and I'm paraphrasing),

> Just so you all know, if you have a king, he's going to rule over you. He'll do things like draft your sons into the army and make your daughters into his servants. He's going to confiscate your fields for his own crops. He's going to take your best animals for his own and tax you to fill his treasury. God has taken care of you first in all things. He doesn't need your

crops, land, kids, animals, or money. An earthly king is going to take care of himself first, and you will suffer at his hand.

Essentially, the warning was that they were going to regret the day they refused a big-K King and asked for a little-k king. They were choosing superficial over supernatural.

But, the leaders ignored the warnings and still demanded a king, so a king they got. His name was Saul. And let's just say that overall, just as God had warned them, things did not go very well. In fact, things ended badly. So, God stepped in. He would allow them to have a king. But this time, He would lead them to who He wanted. This would turn the king campaign on its head, because God doesn't judge like humans.

He sent Samuel to a town called Bethlehem to look for a dad named Jesse, who had a lot of sons. As Samuel was working his way through all those good-looking boys, God spoke to him.

> But the LORD said to Samuel, "Don't judge by his appearance or height. . . . The LORD doesn't see things the way you see them. People judge by outward appearance, but the LORD looks at the heart." (1 Samuel 16:7)

While this is such an amazing statement about God's point of view, it's also kind of scary. We can't just look or act like someone who takes big, bold steps of faith. We can't try to act like we have it all together. There is no fooling God. We must actually live the life that we tell other people to lead and live. For this reason, God never wants us to focus on superficial things. We have to look at what is unseen, beyond the natural, to the things we can only get from a relationship with Christ. That means we have to learn to step away from superficial things and submit ourselves as servants to the supernatural work of Jesus. We don't conform to the world any longer, but take steps toward the things of God.

Now, I totally get that the word *supernatural* has all sorts of odd implications these days, a lot of them negative in our culture. But for our purposes here in a biblical context, we simply mean a life that is *far above* the natural. The *super*-natural. In Jesus's trials, He spoke of this different realm to Pilate:

> My kingdom is not of this world. If My kingdom were of this world, My servants would fight, so that I should not be delivered to the Jews; but now My kingdom is not from here. (John 18:36 NKJV)

Another way to say this might be, "If my kingdom were natural, my people would fight. But because my kingdom is *super*natural, there is another plan, a higher way."

The step for today is realizing that when God is trying to give us the supernatural, we should no longer settle for the superficial.

Next-Step Questions

Why do you suppose our culture is so addicted to the superficial things in life?

_____

_____

How can knowing God's Word, like today's verse of 1 Samuel 16:7, help you understand the supernatural perspective of the Kingdom of God?

_____

_____

Moving out of the superficial to the supernatural, what is your one step of faith to take today?

_____

_____

We **WALK** in
the natural
but **LIVE** in
the supernatural.

STEP

32

___

Frustration to Fulfillment

I love Luke 2, where we find the Christmas story. But one of my favorite passages there often gets overlooked: the story of Simeon. In fact, more than once I've gotten choked up reading the ten verses that tell us about his commitment. Verse 25 gives us some amazing info about this man:

- He was righteous and devout, meaning he had a good reputation with God and the people in the community.
- He was waiting for the Messiah to come to rescue Israel.
- The Holy Spirit was upon him and promised that he would see the Messiah before he died. (Remember, this was well before Acts 2, when the Holy Spirit came upon the disciples.)

The Jewish people in that day were awaiting the Messiah to come to rescue them. But they were looking for a king or warrior with a presence and power to overthrow the Roman rule. The last thought would be for Him to arrive as a baby. Yet, because Simeon was led by the Holy Spirit, he was able to discern the truth.

Meanwhile, because Mary and Joseph were faithful to God, they did what they were supposed to do as Jewish parents and brought their baby boy to the temple for His presentation. They went to make their sacrifices and offerings. What happened next was a divine intersection.

> Simeon was there. He took the child in his arms and
> praised God, saying,
> "Sovereign Lord, now let your servant die in peace,
>   as you have promised.
> I have seen your salvation,
>   which you have prepared for all people.
> He is a light to reveal God to the nations,
>   and he is the glory of your people Israel!" (Luke
>   2:28–32)

Do you think Simeon was ever frustrated or grew weary that he didn't know when this event would take place but was just given an invitation to wait? Do you think he had a moment when he might have argued with the Holy Spirit, as in, "God, really? A newborn? Are you sure?" It would take a huge amount of faith to believe this little baby was the Messiah who had come to save His people. But it appears Simeon wholeheartedly trusted God in this, believing that He would fulfill His purpose.

What about Mary and Joseph's reaction to this man taking their son and blessing Him? "Jesus' parents were amazed at what was being said about him" (Luke 2:33).

But, Simeon had more to say, specifically a difficult message for Mary:

> Then Simeon blessed them, and he said to Mary, the baby's mother, "This child is destined to cause many in Israel to fall, and many others to rise. He has been sent as a sign from God, but many will oppose him. As a result, the deepest thoughts of many hearts will be revealed. And a sword will pierce your very soul." (Luke 2:34–35)

Let's take a step back and think about this moment. We aren't told how long Simeon had been waiting to see Jesus. But we have to assume by the wording that it had been a while. And we all know how hard it is to remain faithful while you have been waiting on something important for a long time. I certainly do. It is not hard for faithfulness to fall to frustration.

As I first told you in Step 5, when our family decided to answer God's call for me to go into music, we sold over half of what we owned, and I started doing odd jobs so I'd be free to travel as needed. We also bought a single-wide mobile home, or a trailer, as they call them. That little mobile home went through torrential downpours from hurricanes. We brought our kids home from the hospital to our trailer. No one ever looked at where we lived and said, "Wow, man, you guys have made it!" But that trailer was home to our family.

Still, we hoped for something more. Let's be real: living in a small single-wide can be frustrating for a growing family. When we bought our mobile home, we had a bedroom for us, and one each for our son and daughter. A few years later, our son Seth was born, and we brought him home to the trailer. For the years between his birth and building our home, he was our little nomad. He moved around between bedrooms without a place of his own. Eventually, we moved a twin bed into Noah's room for him to sleep there. But he never had his own room. And even though the rest of us did, we had to learn how to peacefully coexist (for the most part) in tight quarters.

So, for five years, because we didn't have a TV in our bedroom (we no longer had the space for it), my wife and I would lie there at night and look at house plans together. Like so many couples, we wanted the American dream of building our own home someday. Finally, by the end of 2019, everything lined up and the house we had designed room by room in our minds and hearts was constructed. Because of how far the Lord had brought us and how long we had dreamed together, for probably the first two or three months of being in our new home, my wife would find me, or I would find her, sitting in one of the rooms, alone, crying out of gratitude. We had waited and planned and dreamed and prayed for this for so long.

Seth was six when we moved to our new home. In that house, he got his own room, and we let him design what he wanted it to look like. For the first time in his life, he was able to decide what hung on the walls and what to put where. Obviously, he was grateful to finally have a space to call his own.

Earlier this year, assuming what his answer would be, I asked Seth which he liked better—the trailer or this house. He surprised me when he said, "Our trailer." I paused to let that sink in, then a bit puzzled, I asked, "Why?"

As serious as he could be, he stated, "Because that's where all my memories live. That's where I learned to read. That's where I learned to ride a bike. That's where Noah and I got to share a room. So many things."

While our new house was being built, it was easy for the rest of our family to start to get frustrated with living in the trailer where we had all been for years. We couldn't wait to leave and get into the new home. But, for Seth, he was living a life of fulfillment right where he was, with no knowledge or expectation that there could be anything better. He was happy being with our family in the only home he had ever known.

One of the biggest blessings to come from that experience is that as a family we now have a mutual understanding of the power and beauty of waiting on God for what He can bring in His time. Often, God making us wait is just His protection to get us ready for our assignment. Another great example is this: I was so much more grateful to have a record deal at thirty-three than I would have ever been at twenty-three!

Whatever you may be waiting for today—a house, a spouse, a baby, a career, or a calling—consider that God is building something inside you so that whenever you do receive it, you'll have so much more room in your heart to be grateful for the blessing He gives. When God delivers whatever we have been hoping and praying for, when we watch Him keep His promises, we get to celebrate and experience the gratitude of seeing something special come to life. If we were handed every single thing we ever wanted too soon, we'd lose that opportunity. That doesn't mean waiting is ever easy. I'm sure Simeon grew tired of watching for the Messiah.

In your own moments of frustration, know that you are not alone. God has a definite plan and purpose for your life. But the frustration can become an opportunity to teach us patience as we wait on the good gifts He has promised. That's exactly what makes so many in today's culture stay frustrated with life. But when God teaches us how to wait, when we learn to receive the patience and peace of God, we can find real gratitude and fulfillment.

Next-Step Questions

On a scale of one to ten, how would you rate yourself on being able to wait? Explain your number.

_____

_____

For whatever you are hoping for today, why do you think God may be having you wait? How might you feel when it is fulfilled?

_____

_____

To move from frustration to fulfillment, what is your one step of faith to take today?

_____

_____

> With God, waiting is
> **PROTECTION**,
> prior to **PROVISION**.

STEP

33

Stumbling to Standing

In Step 1, I talked about a baby's first steps. For my wife and me, all three of our kids were unique in the way they started to walk. With the first two only being twenty-two months apart, we really saw the difference. My first son was, well, a little lazy at first. He knew we loved him, and he trusted us enough to see that we were going to eventually bring him anything he needed. With two of us to care for him and no other kids yet, we gave in to that strategy for a while. But, once we started to force his little hand, he wasn't too excited about having to figure out how to go get whatever he wanted. Couple that with the fact he also didn't like to get hurt from all the spills involved in learning to walk, and as a result, he was reluctant to take his first steps and held off as long as possible.

My daughter, Hannah, however, was a different story. She learned to roll around before she could crawl. But, as soon as she could crawl, she wanted to try to walk. As soon as she could walk, she was trying to run. And falling down and getting a little bump or bruise was, to her, just part of the price paid to get where she wanted to go.

Here's what we learned as parents with two very different children taking their first steps: it's just as stressful to have a child who is super-scared to take a step, afraid of getting hurt as it is to try to manage a daredevil who is constantly putting him- or herself in harm's way. You end up spending the same time and energy either way, whether you're providing or protecting.

For Christ-followers, we are all just as different, due to personality, background, and makeup. Some of us will take huge risks of faith and try to run when we need to just focus on our walk. Others have to test the waters and be certain before ever stepping out to try what God wants. But, regardless of our approach to walking in faith with Him, here's the reality we constantly face: Because of sin, we are going to trip, by our own doing or someone else's. We're going to stub our toes because we walk where we aren't supposed to go or we just aren't paying attention to where we are. We're going to stumble, fighting to keep our balance. But, we're bound to fall, and sometimes that is going to hurt—maybe even injure someone else in the process, intentional or not.

The bottom line: to walk in freedom, we have to accept the fact that in learning to stand, we are going to stumble. Along the way, like a Good Father, we have to keep in mind His goal is for us to learn how to stand—and stand strong—and then, under His grace, get back up and move forward. Before we can ever "take a stand for Him," we must learn to simply stand.

One of the first problems we have to overcome when we stumble and fall is knowing God doesn't want us to wallow on the ground in our mistakes and sin. Jesus took care of our debt and penalty. We don't have to pay for anything, because He has already taken care of that. His grace and provision allow us to ask for forgiveness, get back up, and go.

After we are "born again," as John 3 states, we aren't supposed to rely on our own strength or trust in our own power. When we stumble, no matter how often, He will be right there to help us, whether that is to find our balance or, if we have fallen, lift us up to walk again. We are to trust that He will be there to help us take those steps, again and again and again. That's how we will learn to move in the freedom God has given us as we walk in this fallen world.

We have to also keep in mind that, for many reasons, some people will try anything and everything to trip us up and keep us from taking *any* steps of faith. But the beauty of a relationship with Jesus is that when we stumble, when we fall, and even when we get hurt by the traps in this world, He can teach us how to stand back up. As we grow and mature, He can and will show us ways to avoid the traps the next time. He has made a way for us to move *beyond* those things, to get *past* those things, to get *through* those things. Sometimes, we will have to walk through a dark valley to get where we need to go. Other times, we may experience the mountaintop to get there. But valley, peak, or anywhere in between, He is always leading us, walking with us.

In Ephesians 6, we discover that God has given each one of us a uniform, so to speak. (I first mentioned this passage in the introduction.) One that can't be seen physically but that is very real. This uniform is available to all believers and can protect us not only in stumbles and falls, but also from spiritual attacks. It can also keep us standing up for Him, as the passages states. Take a look at Paul's description of what God provides us:

> Be strong in the Lord and in his mighty power. Put on all of God's armor so that you will be able to stand firm against all strategies of the devil. For we are not fighting against flesh-and-blood enemies, but against evil rulers and authorities of the unseen world, against mighty powers in this dark world, and against evil spirits in the heavenly places.
>
> Therefore, put on every piece of God's armor so you will be able to resist the enemy in the time of evil. Then after the battle you will still be standing firm. Stand your ground, putting on the belt of truth and the body armor of God's righteousness. For shoes, put on the peace that comes from the Good News so that you will be fully prepared. In addition to all of these, hold up the shield of faith to stop the fiery arrows of the devil. Put on salvation as your helmet, and take the sword of the Spirit, which is the word of God. (Ephesians 6:10–17)

Eventually, in all areas of life, instead of stumbling, we can learn how to "stand firm." And, in His power, many times we will run and gain ground for His glory. I'll never forget my sense of joy as a parent watching my daughter go from crawling to standing, standing to walking, and walking to running. Just imagine how pleased our Heavenly Father must be when we hand over to Him anything that makes us stumble in exchange for His strength to stand firm.

Next-Step Questions

In your life right now, what tends to cause you to trip and stumble spiritually? Explain.

_____

_____

Where do you sense you are being called to "be strong in the Lord and in his mighty power"? Explain.

_____

_____

To take a stand, what is your one step of faith to take today?

_____

_____

Walking in worship
ALLOWS
standing in strength.

Mess to Message

In 2019, I went to perform a show that I had booked with a ministry called Ground 40 in Monroe, North Carolina, a suburb of Charlotte. I didn't know anything about the organization or the man who ran it. I was asked to play and lead worship as part of an event they had planned for men who were graduating from their program.

I will never forget waiting in a dressing room and suddenly hearing the sound of guys singing to the Lord at the top of their lungs. Immediately, I went out to see what was going on. It had never been my experience to hear men's voices worshiping that loud. As I stood in the back and watched, they played video testimonies of many of the men, all talking about the power of Christ and how they had been set free from addiction. Broken yet unashamed men talking about finding freedom in Christ.

After that, many of them were baptized. I saw grateful families in tears, watching a miracle take place before them—one they had obviously prayed many years to see. Husbands, fathers, sons, and brothers who could have easily been dead but were now being born again, brought to new life. Before long, I was in tears too. By the time it was my turn to get up and sing, I knew I was a part of something extraordinary.

That night began a relationship and ministry partnership with Ground 40 and Wesley Keziah. In fact, the idea for this book came from conversations that Wesley and I had about producing resources for people to understand how to walk in freedom. Because in reality, we are all addicted to sin, however that might manifest in each of us individually.

Wesley graciously agreed to share his testimony with us for this step:

> I was born into a broken home. By the time I was about thirteen, I began smoking marijuana. The first time I experienced cocaine was when a joint was laced with it. Once I knew what cocaine could do, I went straight to that drug. Cocaine led to crack. At nineteen, I got on oxy for a back injury, and I was hooked. That led to methamphetamines. By the age of twenty-one, I was doing heroin. I ended up losing a lot of friends to overdoses. Some of those friends followed me down that road. It's really painful to watch your friends lose their lives because of something you introduced them to.
>
> By the time I was twenty-three, I had walked away from my wife and children. My father died from a self-induced heart attack after taking a

mixture of alcohol and Xanax. When I found him, I just thought he had passed out again. After all the chances he'd been given, this time his addiction won. Then my brother died in a car accident, which really sent me over the edge.

After all that trauma, I spiraled out of control. Multiple times, I overdosed and had to be brought back with doses of Narcan from paramedics. My ten-year addiction to heroin led to arrest after arrest for possession, theft, and resisting arrest. By 2014, on my eighty-second arrest, I was taken to the county jail. I had lost everything—my family, my home, my life, and then my freedom.

But in that same jail cell that had me locked away and had immediately put a stop to my drug use, two chaplains cared enough about this mess of a man, what so many people would consider a "lost cause," and shared the Good News of the gospel with me. It made sense. It felt right. I had fallen way past the bottom, and the only place to look was up. That's when these ministers introduced me to Jesus. The Only One who can save, heal, set free, and put us on a true path to freedom in our bodies, minds, hearts, souls, and spirits.

As of this writing, I am seven and a half years sober. My family is restored—my wife, my three sons, and my daughter. God not only granted me salvation and freedom, but He placed a calling on my life to help guys just like I was—hopeless, homeless, whose lives are a mess. We started Ground 40—an addiction recovery program, right in the same city where I caused so much damage to myself and others. Today, my name is connected to hope and healing, all because of Jesus. We are a ministry that helps men find recovery and stay out of prison and out of addiction. Today, the same policemen who once arrested me now call for me to go talk to a guy in one of their jail cells.

I'm Wesley Keziah. Once, when my life was in my own hands, I was a mess. Today, with my life securely in the hands of Christ, I have a message to share with anyone who will listen. In Christ, you can walk in freedom.

There was a man we first discover in the Bible, in Acts. He wasn't a drug addict. He had never been arrested. In fact, he was a pedigreed Jewish man with a stellar reputation among the religious. But, look at his first mention at the stoning death of Jesus's disciple, Stephen.

> They rushed at him and dragged him out of the city and began to stone him. His accusers took off their coats and laid them at the feet of a young man named Saul.
>
> As they stoned him, Stephen prayed, "Lord Jesus, receive my spirit." He fell to his knees, shouting, "Lord, don't charge them with this sin!" And with that, he died. (Acts 7:57–60)

The religious zealot Saul hated the threat of what Jesus had created so much that he singlehandedly decided to stop anyone who followed Him.

Saul was one of the witnesses, and he agreed completely with the killing of Stephen.

A great wave of persecution began that day, sweeping over the church in Jerusalem; and all the believers except the apostles were scattered through the regions of Judea and Samaria. (Some devout men came and buried Stephen with great mourning.) But Saul was going everywhere to destroy the church. He went from house to house, dragging out both men and women to throw them into prison. (Acts 8:1–3)

From the outside, Saul's life didn't look like a mess, but his heart certainly was. But, just like Wesley, Jesus came after him.

Meanwhile, Saul was uttering threats with every breath and was eager to kill the Lord's followers. So he went to the high priest. He requested letters addressed to the synagogues in Damascus, asking for their cooperation in the arrest of any followers of the Way he found there. He wanted to bring them—both men and women—back to Jerusalem in chains.

As he was approaching Damascus on this mission, a light from heaven suddenly shone down around him. He fell to the ground and heard a voice saying to him, "Saul! Saul! Why are you persecuting me?"

"Who are you, lord?" Saul asked.

And the voice replied, "I am Jesus, the one you are persecuting! Now get up and go into the city, and you will be told what you must do." (Acts 9:1–6)

Saul was so religious that he believed he was doing the will of God by eliminating the followers of this rebel called Jesus. But, he ended up so radically transformed and freed by Christ Himself that he changed his name to Paul. Outside of the handful of disciples, no one is more responsible for the spread of the gospel to the known world—Jew and Gentile—than this murderer-turned-messenger.

No matter our story, our sinful lives are a mess. Our hearts are far from God. Our minds are self-focused. Our spirits are separated from our Creator. But, for every mess, there can be a message. And for every "mess" who believes, God can create a messenger who can change the world—one heart at a time, one step at a time.

Next-Step Questions

In your own life today, where is there still a mess in need of God's help?

_____

_____

What message do you feel God has called you to share?

_____

_____

As God's messenger, what is your one step of faith to take today?

_____

_____

No matter the *SIZE*
of your mess,
God *KNOWS*
how to clean it up.

35

Retracing Your Steps

A s we wrap up the past six days, I want to start with a few questions: How do you know when your life has changed? Is it when you feel like you understand something for the first time? Or when you come to think differently about an issue? Or is it when you realize a godly quality has become second nature to you, a part of your everyday life? Or that something is no longer a part of your life because you have successfully stopped? To repeat, how do you know when you've truly changed?

One of the most difficult truths to understand and accept as we grow in Christian maturity is the difference between being and doing. For example, my wife wants me to *be* her husband, not just do husband duties. My kids want me to *be* their dad, not just do some dad things. What's the difference? The intent and attitude of the heart. Whether I'm with my family or out on the road, I want to be a great husband

and father in a 24-7 role. I want to *be* and *do* for my family because of my deep love and commitment to them.

So, here's how *do* connects to *be* in our faith. How do my wife and kids know my heart for them? How do they know how much I love them? Words are important, of course, but my actions are crucial to being who I am. The same is true for us all in our relationship with Jesus. Do we just feel like we have to *do* Christian activities? Go to church. Give money. Read the Bible. Or are we to be a child of God, a follower of Christ, and then our *dos* will match up with that unique identity? We want to *be* and *do* out of our love for and commitment to Him.

> [Jesus said,] "All who love me will do what I say. My Father will love them, and we will come and make our home with each of them. Anyone who doesn't love me will not obey me. And remember, my words are not my own. What I am telling you is from the Father who sent me. (John 14:23–24)

One of our goals in taking new steps to walk in freedom is to match up being a child of God with doing God's will in a relationship with Jesus through the power of the Holy Spirit. The doing is simply an overflow of being. With that truth in mind, take a few minutes to review Steps 29 through 34, moving toward the following:

- growing in your relationship with Jesus, not focusing on the rules
- working on being submissive to God's will, not your own selfish desires and ambitions

- embracing the supernatural and letting go of the superficial
- removing the frustration we can so easily feel in this life to find fulfillment in God's will
- learning from every stumble to allow the Lord to help you and teach you how to stand
- inviting Christ to turn every mess in life—past and present—into His message

Retracing Your Steps Questions

What was the easiest step for you to take this week?

_____

_____

What was the hardest step you took this week?

_____

_____

Name *all* the steps of faith you chose to take this week.

_____

_____

What can you carry out of this week into the rest of your life?

_____

_____

Moments to Momentum

At eighteen years old, I became a youth pastor at a small country church a mile from my parents' house. We started out with seven students in a small room at the back of the church. With a passion to teach God's Word and only a few years older than the teenagers I had been put in charge of, we spent the first two years growing up together, learning to love Jesus. By the age of twenty and with me now married, our group had grown to thirty students, and we moved to the fellowship hall.

I realized that to make our Wednesday nights feel special and engaging for that precious hour, I had to change my strategy. When I asked the students for ideas, their resounding request was for someone to lead worship before I taught. Just one problem: no one knew how to play guitar and sing. No one even had a guitar.

Deciding what could be a cool ministry and a positive outlet for them to learn to play, I talked with my pastor and bought a cheap guitar to present to my students. But, as often happens with teenagers, they quickly lost interest in learning. So now, whenever I was in my office, I felt like that guitar, sitting in the corner on the stand, was staring me down. Bottom line: we still needed someone to lead worship, and I was the only one who hadn't given it a shot.

After two months of playing the same four chords over and over, I finally worked up the nerve to play one song on a Wednesday night: "Open the Eyes of My Heart." They loved it! After a few weeks and some complaints and requests to add another song, I started learning more.

Next, I decided to try writing some original Christian songs to go along with my Bible teaching. I was surprised when the group connected with *my* music.

Then, something happened I didn't see coming. A youth ministry buddy asked me to sing my songs for his group. Then that friend told another and then another. Soon, I was going around singing at churches. (I mostly went for free, which was a good deal for my friends, so they didn't have to pay a "real" band.)

I stayed in student ministry for seven more years while also writing and leading worship all around southeast Texas. And then God began to change what faithfulness looked like in our family's life. Places in my heart once reserved for teaching and preaching were being replaced by leading worship and writing music. I was terrified because I live in an unincorporated township of two thousand where you either graduate and go to work at a chemical plant, or you go away and get a degree. Music was *not* an option where I live. So, if this was really God's will, He would be leading us into the wilderness.

So, we started taking the steps of faith I shared with you in Step 5. Besides our sacrifices together and what I did to make ends meet, my wife's elementary school teacher pay became our main income as our family trusted Jesus with all we had. Within a few years, I was leading worship all summer at youth camps, playing at coffee shops and churches in my area, and continuing to write and record music. Our local Christian station in Beaumont, Texas, started playing a few of my songs. (More on that in an upcoming step.) I also began to open for artists touring through Houston.

One of the first was Phil Wickham, an incredibly talented songwriter and worship leader. He was so kind to spend time talking with me. Afterward, he and his road manager, Brandon, asked if I'd want to open for him again, and, of course, I agreed.

Nearly a year later, Brandon called me to open for Phil in Tyler, Texas. I'd never played in that area and couldn't wait. On the day of the concert, I arrived at the church, set up my gear, and did my sound check. Now, Phil had played a show in Pittsburgh the night before, so they would be taking four flights throughout the day and finally drive to Tyler that afternoon. After a couple of updates throughout the day, we found out fifteen minutes before start time of the sold-out show that Phil wasn't going to make it.

As I heard the crowd chanting Phil's name, the pastor asked if I would play the entire show. I nervously agreed. When the concert emcee, who didn't know me at all, welcomed everyone, he announced that Phil was not coming. He then introduced me as "The Michael Taylor Band." As

I walked out with my acoustic guitar strapped around my neck, whispering prayers, something happened that I will never forget: the presence of God met us there. I launched into my first song and, from there, proceeded to play everything I knew and told any story that God laid on my heart. That night, we laughed, we cried, and we worshiped together.

The next day, Brandon called me and asked, "What did you do last night? They're telling us what a great time it was. We'd like you to do some shows with us."

Well, that led to Phil introducing me to his manager, who then introduced me to a record label, who then introduced me to a Christian booking agency. That led to me signing with all three. One crazy night changed my family's life forever.

As wild as it sounds, what God used to eventually move me from student ministry into music ministry was a guitar I bought for the kids at my church to learn to play. I thought it had nothing to do with me. But, my testimony just goes to show that you never know what God might use. We can be directed by His Spirit when we have no idea what we are doing.

The day I walked in to sign my first record contract in Nashville, they had also scheduled my first cowriting session with a full-time Christian songwriter, Jeff Pardo. He began to tell me about an idea he had: "There's never been a moment that I was not loved by You." I immediately resonated with the thought that no matter what we go through, God always loves us. His unconditional love is constant. We wrote the song in an hour and a half. To this day, I've never written anything that quickly.

The title of the song was "Never Been a Moment." I will never forget sitting alone in my car, listening to the finished track for the first time. I began to weep as I realized the song was written 100 percent out of pure gratitude for God's overwhelming faithfulness to me, my family, and our story.

I thought back to the day when I accepted the truth about Jesus for myself at ten years old, staring down at red carpet, sitting beside Mrs. Albritton at Vacation Bible School, filling out a card. Then the day when I was seventeen in Newton, Texas, at East Texas Baptist Encampment when I led my cousin Bryan to the Lord during a service. In that moment at the altar, I prayed, "Lord, please let me do this for the rest of my life . . . every day." I knew I was called to minister to people in His name.

I thought back to becoming a youth pastor at eighteen. Getting married. And, yes, to that guitar staring at me from the corner of my office and "Open the Eyes of My Heart." Then to the tough decision to follow God's call into Christian music. I recalled every divine moment as I was sitting there listening to "Never Been a Moment," knowing my life was a testimony to that truth.

There has "never been a moment" when God hasn't held my family and me in His arms. There has "never been a moment" when He didn't show Himself to be *exactly* who He says He is. There has "never been a moment" when He hasn't been, as the song says, "Our Rock, our Peace, our All-consuming, heart-pursuing, grace-extending, never-ending Love."

God delivers moments that may seem like nothing at the time, but when we look back later, we can see the amazing momentum He created with it all. Trying to explain that concept of how God works in our lives to a nonbeliever is like trying to explain the wind to someone who has never been outside. You have to experience it to understand. Yet,

He wants us to use all those moments to gain His momentum to press on and walk in freedom, sharing what He alone can do in our lives.

God's love shown to us in the little moments brings us into His momentum where He works in big ways. Let's close with both the New Living and The Message versions of Philippians 1:6.

> And I am certain that God, who began the good work within you, will continue his work until it is finally finished on the day when Christ Jesus returns. (NLT)

> There has never been the slightest doubt in my mind that the God who started this great work in you would keep at it and bring it to a flourishing finish on the very day Christ Jesus appears. (MSG)

Next-Step Questions

Reflecting on your own life, write down some of your highlights, the moments you can see now when God was at work.

_____

_____

How has God used all your moments to create His momentum? What has He created in you or where has He taken you from that first moment of faith to today?

_____

_____

Reflecting on your own moments created by His momentum, what is your one step of faith to take today?

_____

_____

> There's never been a moment
> I was not held inside Your arms
> And there's never been a day when
> You were not who You say You are.
>
> —FROM THE SONG "NEVER BEEN A MOMENT"
> BY MICAH TYLER AND JEFF PARDO

Random Chance
to Real Change

So far in my music career, the song I wrote and released that has affected the most people and gotten the biggest response, literally all over the world, is "Different," a song I cowrote with my friend Kyle Lee. Here's why I believe it has had such an impact: Everyone wants to change. Everyone wants to be different. They just don't know how.

Like the majority of my songs, this one was born out of my own experience. Being honest, out of my own pain. When I was sixteen years old, I went through a season of depression. I had a bully in my life. An enemy I hated. Every time I saw him or had to deal with him in any way, he drove me crazy and made me furious. His taunts constantly rang in my ears. To this day, I have never been bullied harder in my entire life than by this guy. Every day was a battle to get through and survive his abuse.

The bully's name? Micah. *Yeah, me.* I've never had anyone in my life be meaner than I was to myself as a teenager.

Every morning, my bully stared me down in the mirror. I hated everything about myself. I hated the way I looked and the way I talked. I hated my clothes. I hated how I thought and what I thought about. All I wanted was to be like everybody else. Yes, I was a believer. I knew Jesus. But, I would look at other people, and think, *If I could just have that or be like that or look like that, I would be happy.*

When I looked at how I was created, I thought it was a punishment from God. I remember talking to Jesus and saying, "Why would you do this to me? You could have made me anyone else, and I'm stuck with *this*?"

The house where I grew up in Texas was built in the '70s. The ceiling in my room had these unique designs pressed into the plaster that created a pattern of circles. They kind of looked like big vinyl records. There were probably fifty circles in each, going from the outside to the center. Every day when I came home from school, if my parents asked, "How was your day?" I'd always answer, "It went great." But, it was never great. Far from it. I would go into my room, close the door, throw down my backpack, lie on the bed, and stare at that ceiling.

I would pick one of those circles, starting with the outside ring, and use them to count all the reasons I hated myself that day. Like, "Walking into school this morning, I tripped and looked so stupid. That's one." I would go through my entire day, recalling every single situation where I felt ugly or stupid or less than someone else and attached it to one of the circles. "When I walked up to my friends at school with five of them standing there, three said 'Hi,' but two seemed to ignore me. I know they can't stand me. That's two." Some days I got halfway into the circle, while on the really bad days, I reached all the way to the center.

But my life was changed when a new youth pastor named Kyle came to our church. For his first six months, that guy would not leave me alone. He would see me on Sunday morning and say, "Hey, Micah, you should come to youth group Wednesday night." At that point, our family was Sunday morning–only church people. Nothing else. But eventually, my cousin Amber went to youth camp. She came back and told me how incredible the week had been. She insisted I come with her on Wednesday nights to the student ministry meeting. That first night, Kyle taught a message about how Jesus loved us enough to die on the cross for us—exactly as we are. That message shook me to my sixteen-year-old core. I remember thinking, *Yeah, I want that. I understand You love me. It's hard for me to accept You loving me exactly like I am. After all, I hate how I am. Why do You love that?*

Of course, getting rid of my bully certainly wasn't an overnight fix, but I really did start to pray things like, "So, I don't want to become self-absorbed or anything, but I would like to be able to be in the same room with myself and be OK. I'd be good with that."

Eventually, God revealed this to me: "If you are going to love other people who are my creation, then since I created you, too, how can you show love to others and hate yourself?"

I wasn't a bad kid. I wasn't doing rebellious things. I had loving parents who walked alongside me and tried to be patient and encouraging to a very insecure teenager. But, here's the other side of the story: while I made some good strides in self-esteem and eventually stopped hating myself, I turned into a very insecure thirty-three-year-old who still compared myself to everyone. "Why can't I sing like him? Why can't I write songs like that? Why can't I look like that guy?"

Finally, the Lord broke through to me: "You are who you are supposed to be. You are uniquely, wonderfully, purposefully, functionally made. I have plans for you, and I have something specific for you. I love you, and I want you to write songs from *you*."

I think the reason that "Different" has affected so many people is because I wrote it from such a deep, personal place. I didn't write the song to get on an album. I wrote it for myself, for that kid trying to get past the bully in the mirror. But the song ended up being the one that convinced the record label to sign me, which led to the song being released.

I've gotten letters from people who heard it in a hospital room when hope seemed impossible to find. From people on their way to divorce court who had to pull their car over and pray for God to change their hearts to stay in their marriage. In a prison, where the song came on the radio in a women's unit, and suddenly, the women turned it up and all sang together, "I want to be different. I want to be changed," at the top of their lungs. Then, when the song stopped on the radio, they just keep singing the chorus to each other. In a hut in Africa where a guy was playing the song on an acoustic guitar and singing it to his village.

For a long time, the world has tried to teach us that we were created by random chance. Whether from primordial ooze or apes, we somehow evolved into who we are as a species. No intention, no design, and certainly no love. Believing that worldview, it's no wonder we struggle to care about human life or believe there is any sort of purpose in our lives. That's why no matter our age, so many of us are still just sixteen-year-old kids in our minds and hearts who need to realize that God made us exactly who we're supposed to be. We all need to stop wanting to be someone else, or even a better version of ourselves, and pray, "I want to look more like You, Jesus. Don't turn me into anyone else, unless it's You. When people see me, Lord, I want them to see You. I want to experience real change."

> You made all the delicate, inner parts of my body
> > and knit me together in my mother's womb.
> Thank you for making me so wonderfully complex!
> > Your workmanship is marvelous—how well I
> > know it.
> You watched me as I was being formed in utter
> seclusion,
> > as I was woven together in the dark of the womb.
> You saw me before I was born.
> > Every day of my life was recorded in your book.
> Every moment was laid out
> > before a single day had passed.
> How precious are your thoughts about me, O God.
> > They cannot be numbered! (Psalm 139:13–17)

Next-Step Questions

What ways have you struggled with identity, insecurity, or any self-hatred, whether years ago or still today? Explain.

_____

_____

Is there anyone or anything you still need to let go of so you can experience real change through Christ?

_____

_____

Believing God has all your days mapped out, desiring real change, what is your one step of faith to take today?

_____

_____

> I wanna be different, I wanna be changed
> 'til all of me is gone and all that remains
> is a fire so bright, the whole world can see
> That there's something different,
> So, come and be different in me
>
> —FROM THE SONG "DIFFERENT"
> BY MICAH TYLER AND KYLE LEE

38

Promise-Maker to
Promise-Keeper

One truth I have discovered and continue to work on daily is that God keeps all His promises. But here's an added element we have to consider: His promises are true even when there is nothing in our lives yet to allow us to see they are true. When we can't yet see His work, we have to trust He is a Promise-Maker but equally a Promise-Keeper.

We can look to the Bible to see evidence of this. We will read promises there that we realize we have already experienced. There will be some we find that help us during the season we are in at the time. And then there are those we have no connection with when we read them but will someday desperately need.

I wrote a song in 2016 with Kyle Lee and Tony Wood, called "Even Then." I had no idea at the time that it would become my "Break Glass in Case of Emergency" song. That's the block-lettered command you find printed on the sealed containers in buildings that house items like fire extinguishers, firehoses, axes, and so on. We pay zero attention to those things *until* an emergency and we suddenly, frantically need them. Much like some of God's promises—we pay zero attention to them in the Bible *until* an emergency and we suddenly, frantically need them.

As cowriters, our goal was crafting a song about all the promises of God that we will need someday. We can't ignore any because we could need any of them at any time. I had the original idea and had written the first few lines sitting in my daughter's bedroom one night. The lyrics talked about the times in life when we experience dark nights, strong storms, rising floods, deep fears, and weak faith. Of course, as a writer, I intend words like *storms* and *floods* to be metaphors, not literal, even though they can be. But the chorus reminds us that God never lets us go and is always with us, no matter what we walk through.

But, over the next few years, my own words in the song came back to me, along with God's promises, when

- the tornado sirens went off on my phone when our family still lived in the mobile home, and we prayed we wouldn't get hit or the wind wouldn't carry it away;
- Hurricane Harvey struck our new house with forty— yes, forty—inches of water and literal flood waters rose, causing damage but not destroying our little mobile home;
- I was standing in a car dealership, trying to buy a used vehicle to go on the road and my mom called to

- tell me that my brother Daniel had been diagnosed with cancer; and
- we got the news that my grandmother was diagnosed with cancer.

I suppose if I had any idea what all would be coming our way over the next few years, I would have tried to write a happier song that day! But, the truth is that the difficulty in our circumstances never changes the truth of God's promises. Please allow me to repeat: the difficulty in our circumstances never changes the truth of God's promises. Like I said, He is not just a Promise-Maker, He is a Promise-Keeper.

I want to talk about three specific truths I have experienced regarding God's promises:

Truth #1: We may need God's promises much more than we realize at the time.

As a yong, married youth pastor, I went to a men's retreat with all the guys in our church. My goal was to become better friends with some of the men and learn how to be a godly man. I wanted to know how to be strong and brave as a Christ-follower. But, when the teaching started, I realized the entire focus for the weekend was on how to be a godly father to your children. I remember all the guys from our church crying and talking about how much the teaching was affecting them to be better dads. But, honestly, it was kind of boring to me. When they asked me, "Micah, what did you think about the weekend?" I said, "Guys, I'm so glad it meant so much to you. Who knows? Maybe one day I'll need to know some of this stuff."

As I pulled out of the parking lot at the camp to return home, I called my wife to catch up. Guess what. She told me that she had just done a pregnancy test and it was positive. My immediate thought was, *Why didn't I listen more? Why didn't I take notes? Why did I dismiss the teaching?* But God knew what was about to happen and gave me a clear opportunity to grab hold of promises I was about to need.

Truth #2: We have to pay close attention to what God promises *and* what He doesn't.

Here's an example:

> The Lord is close to the brokenhearted;
>> he rescues those whose spirits are crushed.
> (Psalm 34:18)

I can attest to the fact that when my heart has been broken, I knew that my Savior was close, standing with me. He also eventually pulled me out from the place where my spirit was crushed. But, this promise does not say that our hearts will *not* be broken. It does not say that our spirits will *not* be crushed. This is exactly where so many get confused, because they falsely believe that when God comes into our lives, nothing bad will ever happen to us again.

We can't get angry at God for His lack of protection when our hearts get broken, because He did not promise that. That's why we must pay very close to attention to what the Scripture says and what it does not say. Often, as sinners, we impose our thoughts on God or make assumptions that He never told us. Like any relationship that is growing in the area of trust, with time and experience we can learn how to listen and obey His voice.

Truth #3: Through His promises, God can show us even more of Him than we asked for.

When we were going through the hurricane, I prayed, "God, will you be Protector over my home?" Well, we ended up with damage, which caused me to ask Him, "Why weren't You our Protector? Why would You allow that?" But, as I kept seeking Him, I began to realize He did protect us. Our house didn't fall apart. Yes, we had to replace the floors and some walls, but we were able to stay in our home.

What this also allowed me to see was that while God protected the rest of our house, I also got to know Him as Provider for the part that was damaged. He worked everything out to put our home back together. Now, I didn't ask him to be Provider, just Protector, but He said, "I'm going to let you know who I am in more ways than one. More than you asked Me to show You."

Likewise, when I prayed, "Jesus, will You be Healer to my brother?" Daniel wasn't miraculously healed after I prayed. While we waited for the healing that eventually came the second time, we got to experience Him as Comforter.

When I have wanted one thing in the moment, He has sometimes given me something else first, because He knew as a Perfect Father what I needed more than I did. Because of that I got to experience more of God through what He showed me. Not just as Protector, but as Provider. Not just as Healer, but as Comforter.

We all know what it feels like to have promises broken or for us to break promises to others. But, we serve a God who makes promises and keeps them all. Together, we stand on those, because everything else in this life is built on a temporary and faulty foundation. This world can make a lot of promises, but it cannot keep them. That's why Psalm 18:30–31 remains true in every generation, each day of our lives.

> God's way is perfect.
>> All the LORD's promises prove true. . . .
> For whom is God except the LORD?
>> Who but our God is a solid rock?

Next-Step Questions

Has there been a time in your walk with God when you questioned if He had kept His promise? What happened? (If you feel that is still unresolved, what might God still be able to show you?)

_____

_____

Has there been a time in your walk with God when He fulfilled a promise to you? What happened?

_____

_____

Trusting the One who keeps all His promises, what is your one step of faith to take today?

_____

_____

> Even when it feels like my world is shaken
>
> Even when I've had all that I can take
>
> I know, You never let me go
>
> I know, no matter how it ends
>
> You're with me, even then
>
> —FROM THE SONG "EVEN THEN"
> BY MICAH TYLER, KYLE LEE, AND TONY WOOD

STEP

39

Concealed to Consumed

We gave our youngest child, Seth, a nickname when he was just four years old. We started calling him "The Happy-Maker." Always a super-happy kid who loves to laugh, he's a bit of a natural entertainer. He's also very easy to please. But his absolute favorite thing is to make other people happy. The sadder you appear to be, the more of a challenge you are to him.

Here's an example: Seth would bop into the room, look at me, and ask, "Hey Dad, how are you doing?"

If I said, "Oh, I'm fine," he pressed, "No, how are you doing?"

Then if I answered, "Well, I'm doing pretty good," he asked, "So, are you a little sad?"

If I said, "Maybe a little," he looked at me, perked up, and blurted out, "I think you need a Number 37!"

At that, Seth would come over and give me a very cus-tomized hug. *Embrace* is probably a better word.

Evidently, he had mentally numbered a bunch of differ-ent hugs. Seth sized you up, like a doctor focused on specific symptoms and, on the spot, gave you a prescription for your hug, which he then delivered himself. He offered the hug he felt you needed in the moment—the one that would most help you. "I think you need a Number 14 today" or, "I'm going to give you a Number 6." We had no idea how many of these hugs he had inventoried and numbered, but it was always very convincing and personal.

But, here was the best part to us: after Seth released me from his hug, he always said something like, "There, I bet that's better."

I would usually tell him something like "Yeah, I'm really happy now."

He would grin ear to ear, and say, "Oh, I'm so glad." The look of satisfaction on his face when he saw that he had once again pulled off his job as "The Happy-Maker" was always priceless.

At our core, we all want to feel like we can change the world, don't we? And the best way to do that is one person at a time. Seth got that truth down early. But, here's the other side of the story: as much as I love my son's hugs, if I always relied on him to make me happy, to give me joy and sustain my life in that way, it wouldn't last. It *couldn't* last. Why? Because that is not Seth's job. He is growing up, and as much as I don't want to think so, he could decide to retire completely from the hugging business one day. Yet another reason why my relationship with Christ is so important. He is my only Source of real joy. My son can lift my spirits and elevate my mood any time, but my joy flows from Jesus.

One of my most popular songs is simply titled "AMEN," cowritten with James Andrews and Jeff Pardo. The day it was written, one of the guys started talking about Peter and John in Acts 4 and how Jesus's disciples couldn't get over what He had done for them. They just could not stop talking about Him. They had become consumed by Jesus's love, grace, and mercy, to the point where they couldn't *not* share Him. As we wrote the lyrics and joined up the melody, we discussed how the truth of the gospel is that we have a joy inside that is recurrent. No matter what, it just keeps happening inside of us.

After Jesus's earthly ministry was over and He had died, risen, and ascended to the Father, the Holy Spirit came, just as He promised. The disciples were assigned the mission of going into the world to spread the Word. The religious leaders of the day quickly realized they had not succeeded in snuffing out the Light of the World. In fact, now it was burning as brightly as ever and spreading quickly. Literally, thousands of people were hearing the gospel and believing in Jesus. So, these religious leaders arrested two of the loudest preachers, Peter and John. As they began to question them and hear their answers, a fascinating thing occurred.

> The members of the council were amazed when they saw the boldness of Peter and John, for they could see that they were ordinary men with no special training in the Scriptures. They also recognized them as men who had been with Jesus. . . .

"What should we do with these men?" they asked each other. "We can't deny that they have performed a miraculous sign, and everybody in Jerusalem knows about it. But to keep them from spreading their propaganda any further, we must warn them not to speak to anyone in Jesus' name again." So they called the apostles back in and commanded them never again to speak or teach in the name of Jesus.

But Peter and John replied, "Do you think God wants us to obey you rather than him? We cannot stop telling about everything we have seen and heard."

The council then threatened them further, but they finally let them go because they didn't know how to punish them without starting a riot. (Acts 4:13, 16–21)

So, to recap, the religious leaders said, "Hey, you guys have to quit talking about this so much. We're going to let you go, but you need to quiet down about Jesus, OK?" Their answer was, "How in the world can we keep quiet about something so amazing?"

Galatians 5:1 states, "It is for freedom that Christ has set us free" (NIV). Walking free is not something that we keep concealed. Real freedom is all-consuming. Jesus was never meant to be some sort of secret. Honestly, like Peter and John, we should not be able to get over the things that we have seen and heard either. We want to make sure that others get in on the freedom too.

My son Seth couldn't (and still can't) conceal his happiness. He was consumed and wanted to share it. He wanted to see us experience what he had and was willing to risk some of himself to give it away. As Christ-followers, what kind of people would we be to keep freedom inside of us? To be around people every day who are locked up and not say a word to them, not share with them? If we truly believe that Jesus has changed our lives, why would that not absolutely consume our hearts? As Isaiah 52:7 states, "How beautiful on the mountains are the feet of the messenger who brings good news, the good news of peace and salvation."

Next-Step Questions

Is anything or anyone keeping you from talking about what Jesus has done in your life? Explain.

_____

_____

When was the last time the joy of the Lord overflowed in your life in such a way that you couldn't contain it? Explain.

_____

_____

Deciding the gospel can no longer be concealed and your heart must be consumed, what is your one step of faith to take today?

_____

_____

> How could I hide this joy inside of me?
>
> Amazing grace, oh Lord, how can it be?
>
> Every day of my life, I want the world to see
>
> I can't get over what You've done for me
>
> —FROM THE SONG "AMEN"
> BY MICAH TYLER, JAMES
> ANDREWS, AND JEFF PARDO

STEP

40

Merit to Mercy

The hardest song I have ever written—so far—was "New Today." It's not that the writing took a long time, but it was about what was going on in our lives at the time. As I've mentioned a few times, my brother Daniel had been diagnosed with cancer in 2017. They said the cancer had spread from his colon to his stomach lining and then his liver. They believed it was spreading all over his body. They had given him no longer than two years to live. After being on the most vicious chemo they could give him, the doctors were scared he might lose limbs because of how intense the mixture was.

The doctor decided to schedule exploratory surgery in October 2018. They wanted to go in and take an actual look at the cancer. The problem that would create was that once they stitched him back up, they couldn't do chemo for a while because it would kill all that tissue. For that reason, the surgery was a risk, but they wanted to see where the cancer had either spread or decreased from the treatments.

The week before the surgery, I had come to Nashville from our home in Texas to write new songs. As I have previously stated, my goal is to always write from an honest place and align with God's Word. I personally believe I have to have spiritual integrity in the songs for listeners to hear from a Christian worldview and also see God in the midst of their everyday lives.

During that season, I prayed countless times, "God, would You have mercy on my brother? Lord, would You please show Your mercy to my family?" And, finally, because of *everything* we had gone through, I prayed, "Would You just have mercy on me?" Sitting in my car before I walked in to write, I got real with the Lord: "God, it's hard for me to think about writing songs right now. This feels trivial compared to everything that's going on in our family." Then I wiped the tears from my eyes, got out of the car, grabbed my guitar, and walked into the room to meet the two writers I would be working with that day, Colby Wedgeworth and Paul Duncan.

After the usual small talk, I told them, "Today, I need to write a song that could be played at my brother's funeral in a few months . . . or a song of victory over this cancer that we're battling right now. I just need to be reminded of the Lord's mercy."

One of the writers turned to me and quoted Lamentations 3:22–23:

The faithful love of the LORD never ends!
    His mercies never cease.
Great is his faithfulness;
    his mercies begin afresh each morning.

In that moment as we talked openly, I realized there are times when we need mercy and we think that we have to sacrifice everything we have to receive it. We have to figure it all out, as in, "Whatever I have to pray to You, whatever I have to say to You, whatever I have to do for You, whatever I have to be for You, I just want mercy. I just want mercy for my family." Somehow, I was falsely thinking that my own merit, my actions or behavior, would convince God to allow me a little bit of mercy. As if mercy is some kind of reward given for levels of personal sacrifice.

Being reminded in a brand-new way that God's mercy never ends, never stops, and there is a fresh supply available to us every single day was the greatest relief for me. It was like a weight lifted off my chest. I didn't have to do anything to experience God's mercy; it was right there waiting for me to receive. That's how "New Today" was born.

Through the entire journey with Daniel's cancer, I kept telling myself that I didn't need to do anything. I didn't have to go anywhere to find God's mercy. I didn't have to finally arrive at the level where God's mercy lives. I didn't have to beg Him hard enough. I didn't have to ask for it a certain number of times. I didn't have to wear Him down that morning to get mercy. It's never about my goodness and faithfulness, but His. God simply offers us His mercy. We never have to look up and say, "Gee, I sure wish I could have some of that." In fact, He lavishes those things on His children. He's so good that He just makes it available every day because He knows we're going to need it. As our Creator, He knows our needs.

Ten days later when they did the exploratory surgery on my brother to see how extensive the cancer was, they found none. *There was no more cancer!* The doctors had to present his case before the medical board of the hospital. They reported that the only treatment was the chemo. But, when they went in: no cancer, therefore no limb loss. None of the warnings they gave came true. The only thing they could say was that this was a medical miracle.

Mercy!

Daniel's doctors had told him he could never father children, but within a year, he and his wife were pregnant with their daughter. Not only did the Lord restore the things that cancer tried to take away, but He added in abundance on top of that.

Mercy!

For our family, while we respect, appreciate, and pray for the doctors, surgeons, and the treatment plans, God is the only One to whom we can attribute miracles. And mercy!

Merit is all about us and our best efforts. Mercy is receiving something when you have nothing to offer. But mercy is not just some divine gift that we are given; it is an expression of God's great love in the midst of Him meeting our needs.

Now, I firmly believe that Daniel would have either been healed here on this earth to be able to tell his story as a testimony for others, or he would have been taken to a place where cancer would never touch him again: Heaven, where he would be healed forever. Regardless, walking through that first bout of cancer with Daniel, coupled with the writing of an honest song called "New Today," gave me a brand-new understanding and acceptance of God's great gift of mercy. Now that the cancer has returned and those days still come when I realize my need for the mercy of God, I know a gift has already been graciously offered to my family and me through every step: His *new* mercy.

Next-Step Questions

Have you struggled with feeling like you have to earn God's mercy and love on your own merit? Explain.

_____

_____

When have you experienced God's mercy in your own life?

_____

_____

Laying down your merit and accepting God's mercy, what is your one step of faith to take today?

_____

_____

Help me rise like the morning sun
Help me see that Your work's not done
When I'm less than what I want to be
Lord, I need You to keep reminding me
Your mercies are new today

—FROM THE SONG "NEW TODAY"
BY MICAH TYLER, COLBY WEDGEWORTH,
AND PAUL DUNCAN

41

Grief to Grace

I have to remind myself at times that I'm not a "professional Christian." Because I create Christian music for my family's living, it can be hard to not think that way when I write music, travel the world, stand on stages, and sing my songs. But when I find my identity solely in the things I *do*, I miss out on my true passion and highest calling: to *be* a faithful servant. (This can be a struggle for anyone who is paid to do any kind of ministry for a living.)

For this step on our journey, let's address an important topic for me that became a song I love: "I See Grace." The song came about in a cowriting session with Matthew West and Zach Kale. As we settled in and started to share with one another, one of them began to talk about a difficult and heartbreaking situation taking place in his family. It was one of those seemingly hopeless circumstances in which it can become hard to see how God could ever turn things around. You know He can, but you can't see how. But he ended by saying he wanted to look at the entire situation from the perspective of Jesus, not his own, to be able to "see grace" and believe for God's best in the end.

We've all been there, right? We get it. Our hearts can struggle with such deep grief about a circumstance, but we know in faith we need to hang on to God's grace and believe things can change.

Our family has been through a lot these past few years (and we're still walking through at this writing). Through it all, night after night, I've stood on stages to minister and encourage others. Through it all, I've had to learn to balance this walk between grief and grace. And it's never easy.

In Revelation 12:11, John shared the words of Jesus, the Author of grace, as He spoke about the author of grief: "And they have defeated him by the blood of the Lamb and by their testimony." I know that every day the blood of Christ covers my life and I can take my current day-to-day testimony and put it to melody and lyrics. I can honestly share what I'm walking through in any season. But a few years ago, I realized that I was still holding on to some of the guilt and shame from my past mistakes. Whenever I thought about my bad decisions or things that had been done to me, I would experience the hurt all over again and feel the emotional pain. In trying to get past that battle, I came to the conclusion that the closer I get to Jesus and the more I follow alongside Him, the better I am able to see everything from *His* point of view, not mine. I am grateful to say that, today, when I look back at those same mistakes, I just see Jesus's forgiveness of me. I no longer see what I did wrong. I only see His hope, His mercy. *I see grace.* As the old hymn states, "A grace that is *greater* than all our sin."

Now, even when I was unable to allow grace for myself, I had no trouble offering it to others. When I became a youth pastor at just eighteen years old, I felt like I was suddenly held to a higher standard. So, I worked hard to try to follow the rules to meet everyone's expectations. I wanted to make myself look like I was wise and holy by making sure I checked off as many spiritual boxes as possible, to not do the don'ts and do all the dos—something that is not possible at *any* age, no matter what you do for a living.

Being transparent here, I wanted to show the people around me that I didn't even need grace because I was not going to mess up. God's grace was my backup plan. If I didn't nail it, if I didn't figure it out, *then* I could rely on His grace.

How long did that work for me? Not long. I began to realize that relying on His grace is not a weakness. To the contrary, by feeling like I could accomplish some level of "perfection" all by myself, my pride became my weakness. All through this internal struggle, I offered grace to everyone else—*except* for me.

First Corinthians 13:5 tells us that love "keeps no record of being wronged." I realized that I was not tallying up wrongs for anyone else, but I was for my own sin, keeping a record that God wasn't. I was not loving myself the way that He wanted. I was not accepting His grace for me, just for everyone around me. I wanted to try to move past my mistakes, but I constantly attached shame to every sin. That feeling makes any of us want to hide whatever we have done. We feel shame. We feel pain. So we hide. I sure did. Even as a youth pastor.

Over time, through God growing and maturing me, I knew I had to receive and accept His grace, mercy, and hope for me *first*. It's kind of like the airline's emergency rule: put on your oxygen mask first and then help everyone else. I also had to accept being a child of God *before* I was a minister. I had to practice what I was teaching the students in my care. Even as an adult with adult responsibilities, I had to be His child first. And by the age of twenty, when my wife and I got married, my reliance on God's grace had to go even deeper.

Because of what Jesus accomplished on the cross, we were never meant to hold ourselves to some personal unattainable standard. We were never supposed to try to be responsible for our sin. We confess and give it all to God, and He lifts that responsibility off of us with His atonement and sacrifice. Then, we are not left with guilt and shame, but His righteousness. We are only left with the remembrance that Jesus loved us enough to see our sin, step into our lives, and offer grace. The divine exchange of our "filthy rags" for His forgiveness.

But what do we do with the memories of our sin? While we can accept forgiveness, we can't forget. The answer is, we are to learn from those mistakes. Use them to gain the perspective of how God sees the circumstances. Keep no record.

If you are struggling to forgive yourself for something, I want you to consider this question that I had to face: Why are you holding yourself to a higher standard than what God Himself is holding you to? Right now, He is saying, "If you will lay that down, if you will give it to Me, I will forgive all of the sin and set you free." I know, because that's what He told me.

We are denying God and robbing ourselves when we will not allow His full gift of forgiveness for the things we carry. If we hold on to any of it, we are putting ourselves in the place of the Forgiver, when we are only called to be the forgiven. Whether for the first time or the first time in a long time, God wants you to be able to say, "I see grace . . . for me."

Here are two of my go-to Scriptures to remind myself of the grace of God:

> "My grace is all you need. My power works best in weakness." So now I am glad to boast about my weaknesses, so that the power of Christ can work through me. (2 Corinthians 12:9)

> God saved you by his grace when you believed. And you can't take credit for this; it is a gift from God. (Ephesians 2:8)

Next-Step Questions

What has been your most difficult thing to let go of and give to Jesus? Or what are you struggling with right now that you need to give to Him?

_____

_____

Today, what do you need to do to be able to say, "I see grace for me"?

_____

_____

Letting go of grief to receive grace, what is your one step of faith to take today?

_____

_____

> When I left the ninety-nine, You saw the one
>
> And just like that, all my past had been erased
>
> When I look back, I see grace.
>
> —FROM THE SONG "I SEE GRACE"
> BY MICAH TYLER, MATTHEW
> WEST, AND ZACH KALE

STEP

42

Sinner to Saint

As we finish up this deep dive into some of my songs and the biblical truths connected to them, I'm going to make a confession. As I go through the Bible, I tend not to relate so much to the "heroes of the faith" as much as to the guys who just kept messing up. Here's what I mean: we can read stories like Noah, the Ark Builder; Abraham, the Father of Nations; Moses, the Sea Part-er; and David, the Giant Killer. But then we can continue reading to find out the human frailties of these people. Noah had too much to drink and embarrassed himself in front of his family. Abraham had a couple of bouts with deception, particularly when it came to the women in his life. Moses committed murder and had his bad days of disobeying God. And David? Well, we've already covered his issues in Step 11.

We have to continually remind ourselves to respect the folks in Scripture but also keep in mind they were just like us.

One side of the story was that they were all broken people. The other side was how God worked in and through them to accomplish His purposes. In these stories, we see the sinner, the human element, but we also see the saint, the God factor.

The same is true for us today.

As I read these accounts in the Bible repeatedly, I can see life from both sides. Time and again, what I have come to realize is if God can love people like that, then He can love someone like me. And, as I told you yesterday, I finally came to accept the truth that He does.

So, then I have to take that a step further and ask, How in the world could He not love *all* the people around me, even the ones I might struggle to love? We're all just fellow travelers in the faith, trying to walk this journey of freedom together.

One of the most interesting passages in Scripture is Paul's confession of his own internal struggle with those same two sides of himself—the sinner and the saint.

And I know that nothing good lives in me, that is, in my sinful nature. I want to do what is right, but I can't. I want to do what is good, but I don't. I don't want to do what is wrong, but I do it anyway. But if I do what I don't want to do, I am not really the one doing wrong; it is sin living in me that does it.

I have discovered this principle of life—that when I want to do what is right, I inevitably do what is wrong. I love God's law with all my heart. But there is another power within me that is at war with my mind. This power makes me a slave to the sin that is still within me. Oh, what a miserable person I am! Who will free me from this life that is dominated by sin and death? Thank God! The answer is in Jesus Christ our Lord. (Romans 7:18–25)

I don't know about you, but when I read that passage, I think, *Yeah, Paul, I get it! Me too!* With his incredible honesty on this dilemma, I'm most grateful about how Paul closed out his confession. In this human tug-of-war, "the answer is in Jesus Christ our Lord"!

One of the things I had to accept early on as I began to be heard on the radio and sing in front of crowds is that God can use me just as I am to encourage people just like me. I'm not called because I'm a hero of the faith or have anything special over anyone else. Like those people in the Bible, I've simply committed my life to the higher calling of Christ. He's the Difference-Maker.

I want to share a story with you that drove this point home for me. In 2012, I recorded my first album of eight songs I had written. I then took the CD to a DJ, Jeff Roberts, at a nearby Christian station. I asked if he would listen to my songs and tell me if any of them were any good. He graciously agreed, and we met at a restaurant to talk. As we got started with the critique, I saw that he was kind enough to have made notes on each song with some helpful feedback.

As he went through the list, he stopped on one and said, "And this song sounds good on the radio." I smiled and asked, "Really? Do you think it will?" The DJ clarified, "No, it *does*. It *does* sound good. I've already been playing it this past weekend. Have you not heard it yet?"

Now, here was the trick: from where we lived, I had to drive fifteen miles closer to his station to pick up the radio signal in my car. So the next day, he called and told me he was going to play the song in twenty minutes. I jumped in my car and drove to a Walmart parking lot within range to be able to hear it on the radio for the first time.

Over the next year, that DJ played multiple songs from that first record, including one called "Mighty to Love," which became their number one requested song. The following year, the radio station called me to sing at their listener appreciation concert. They packed out a local church with about five hundred people in attendance—the biggest crowd I had played for at that time.

Besides the sheer number of people, I thought the most special part of the night was getting to hear everyone sing along with my songs. But God had another amazing surprise in store for me. One that would set the tone for my ministry moving forward and show me what I always want my music to be about and for—people like us.

After the concert was over, I went back to my table where my CDs were being sold. A young lady walked up and introduced herself. Then she asked, "Can I tell you my story?" I answered, "Sure, love to hear it." She began.

> About a year ago, I started dating a guy, and we were both in a bad place. I ended up getting pregnant. When I told him, he said, "I don't even know you, and I sure don't love you. I don't want anything to do with this. Just get it taken care of." And he was gone. I never saw him again.
>
> So, I went to my parents and told them. They said the same thing the guy did. "We're not helping you. You got yourself into this. Get yourself out of it.

Go to the clinic and get an abortion." So, I made an appointment. On my drive there that day by myself, I was very upset and crying. I had never listened to Christian music before, but I found a station on the dial and turned it up. Then I prayed, "God, would You just say something to me? Please."

Out of nowhere, I heard these words: "You are here and You are strong. You're mighty to save us from all of our wrongs. From the first sunrise to the day the sun falls. You hold us together because You're mighty to love." I pulled over on the side of the road to listen, crying uncontrollably.

She paused for a second as I stood there stunned and fighting back tears. Then she smiled and asked, "Micah, would you like to meet my son?" The young lady turned around, reached down, and held up her three-month-old baby boy to me. That was the moment when I committed not just to penning lyrics and creating melodies, but to offering messages about the truth of the gospel, the answer in Jesus Christ.

In 2022, I wrote and released a song called "People Like Us," a song that encompasses that theme from all those years ago. I want people to know that no matter what they have been through, where they have walked, what they have done, who they have been in the past, or who has hurt them, God's love is always available. Because He is "Mighty to Love," I can say, "God loves people like you, 'cause God loves people like me. A lost and hopeless sinner that mercy has redeemed." Yes, we are sinners, but through Christ, He can create a saint, someone fully surrendered to His ways and His will.

This is a trustworthy saying, and everyone should accept it: "Christ Jesus came into the world to save sinners"—and I am the worst of them all. But God had mercy on me so that Christ Jesus could use me as a prime example of his great patience with even the worst sinners. Then others will realize that they, too, can believe in him and receive eternal life. (1 Timothy 1:15–16)

Next-Step Questions

Does anything from your past or present keep you from walking in freedom? Do you need to take care of anything to make certain you are fully surrendered to Jesus?

_____

_____

Like my testimony, like the young lady in today's story, and like Paul, what do you need to do to arrive at the place where you pray, "God, use me as a prime example of Your great patience with even the worst sinners. Then others will realize that they, too, can believe in You and receive eternal life"?

_____

_____

Believing that God can create saints from sinners, people like us, what is your one step of faith to take today?

_____

_____

It don't matter who you are
It don't matter who you've been
Oh, and if you have forgotten
Let me tell you once again
That God loves people like you

—FROM THE SONG "PEOPLE LIKE US"
BY MICAH TYLER, ZACH KALE, AND JEFF PARDO

Retracing Your Steps

As we begin to wrap up our time together, in this step, I've only given you the review questions, just like you have been working through in the book. As you complete this step and head into the final two, these could be the most impactful and crucial ones in your entire journey, with the hope and goal that you can discover what God is speaking to you in this season of your life.

Retracing Your Steps Questions

What was the easiest step for you to take this week?

_____

_____

What was the hardest step you took this week?

_____

_____

Name *all* the steps of faith you chose to take this week.

_____

_____

What can you carry out of this week into the rest of your life?

_____

_____

WALKING FREE—TO THE FINISH LINE

Derek Redmond had a great career in running track. He held the British record in the 400 meters and won gold medals on the relay team at the World and European Championships. In the 1992 Olympics in Barcelona, in his first round, he posted the fastest time and went on to win his quarterfinal. But in the semifinal, the unthinkable happened. The runner's nightmare occurred. Especially in the biggest race of his career.

In the back straight, 250 meters from the finish line, Derek's right hamstring tore. The excruciating pain gripped his body, and he immediately went from a full sprint to a limp. Finally, he stopped and knelt down on the asphalt as the reality of what had happened hit him. By that point, the other runners had continued on and crossed the finish line.

About that time, Derek rose to his feet and began to hobble forward as fast as his good leg could carry him. His agony and disappointment was made clear by the pained expression on his face. Suddenly, all 65,000 spectators shifted their focus from the finish line back to Derek, who was desperately trying to reach the finish line.

As some officials began to run out toward him, an older man in a T-shirt, shorts, and cap ran down the bleachers and jumped the wall onto the track. Able to get past all the distracted security personnel, he ran to Derek, speaking to him while placing his arm around his waist to offer support on the track. As Olympic personnel in green blazers went out to the two of them, the older man kept waving them off, telling them to leave Derek alone, to allow him to finish with dignity.

Leaning even more on the man, Derek was in tears with his hand over his face, overcome with the tragedy of his injury, but also the standing ovation and cheers of the supportive crowd. Finally, the two men, arm in arm, crossed the finish line, just before medical personnel got to him.

Who was the older man who ran out of the stands and onto the track to get to the hurting runner? Derek's father. The only one who could possibly understand the great sacrifice his son had made to be in the race—and the only one he would allow to come and help him finish his race.

The fascinating fact about this story is that most people cannot tell you who won the gold, silver, or bronze in that Olympic race, because the courage of Derek and the faithfulness of his father became the greater victory that day. No one cared that he finished last, because the more powerful point was that he finished at all! The Olympic Committee released a video of the race with this phrase: "Strength is measured in pounds. Speed is measured in seconds. Courage? You can't measure courage."

Your Father in Heaven is not concerned about your strength or your speed, only your courage. He walks alongside you every moment of every day to lead, guide, and support as you walk in His freedom. Remember, our goal someday is not to hear Jesus say, "Well done, quick and fast runner," but, rather, "good and faithful servant." To hear Him say, "You victoriously walked in the freedom that I died and rose again to give you." In the New Testament, the metaphor of life as a race is not about making sure we win, but that we finish strong and arrive at our ultimate destination: the presence of Jesus.

Along with Matthew West and AJ Pruis, I wrote the song "Walking Free" with Jesus's words in John 8:36 as the inspiration: "So if the Son sets you free, you are truly free." Whether someone has a testimony like I do—raised in a good Christian home and came to Christ as a child in Vacation Bible School—or like the men we featured in the "Walking Free" video whom Jesus saved out of a living Hell, the same freedom through His gift of salvation and mercy is offered.

No matter the Bible story we read in these pages, we saw that all those folks had something in common: they all fell short of the glory of God. The wages of their sin was death. But the gift of God was that He redeemed, reconciled, and gave freedom to all those people.

For each step we have taken together, you have also walked in the same shoes as everyone we have read about. As we near the end of the book, we're also coming to your first step into what I pray will be a new day, a new season in your life. In our time together, you've gotten into a discipline, a routine, a flow of spending time with God and reading His Word. Those practices may be Basic Christianity 101, but they are the keys to continue to walk in freedom throughout your life.

In this journey, however small, big, or bold those steps have been on any given day, some of them may have been hard for you. Maybe some days you felt like you crawled your

271

way through. But regardless, here you are. You're at the end. To that victory, I say, "Well done, my friend!"

The truly beautiful thing here is that this is just the beginning. You and I are going to stumble every single day. We will get knocked down. But the difference now is that's not where we will stay. When we fall down, we will get back up. We never have to go back where we were again. We are not wandering. We are staying the course. We want to make sure that we keep going in the right direction, keep focusing on Jesus one step at a time.

> Walking free
> No more darkness
> Guilt has lost its grip on me
> When Mercy called my name
> Those chains fell at my feet
> and now I'm walking,
> walking, walking free
>
> —FROM THE SONG "WALKING FREE"
> BY MICAH TYLER, MATTHEW
> WEST, AND AJ PRUIS

WRAP-UP REVIEW

This final exercise is to help you look back over the entire book and all your hard work to gain as much insight and wisdom as you can about what God is telling you and where He may be leading you to walk next. Take some time now to go back and review all the Retracing Your Steps reviews: 7, 14, 21, 28, 35, and 43.

As you review your Retracing Your Step answers, work through the following:

Wrap-Up Review Questions:

1. Check for any common threads, patterns, repeat concepts, or issues. What continues to rise to the top and jump out as you read what you wrote throughout all the steps?

_____

_____

2. What did God reveal to you that you might have already known but now see that you need to work on and apply?

_____

_____

3. Was there a new truth (or truths) that God revealed to you that need your full attention?

_____

_____

4. Take a look at all your hardest steps. Which seem lighter now, or which may need more help?

_____

_____

5. What is the biggest truth that God revealed to you in all the steps?

_____

_____

6. Has God called you to some mission or ministry? Be as specific as you can in your answer.

_____

_____

7. Lastly, whom can you come alongside to support walking in freedom? A family member? A friend? Someone in your circles of influence? Maybe you could take someone or a small group through the book and facilitate. You could do this two ways: First, have everyone go through a step and then get together to discuss the content and their answers. Or second, read a day out loud and use the questions to openly discuss.

Whom do you need to put your arm around and either help get into the race or to their finish line?

_____

_____

> We have **FREEDOM** now, because Christ made us free. So stand **STRONG**.
>
> —Galatians 5:1 (NCV)

BEGINNING A RELATIONSHIP WITH GOD THROUGH JESUS CHRIST

Maybe at some point as you have been going through *Walking Free*, you have had the question, "So how do I begin a relationship with God?" If you have, then first, we encourage you, if at all possible, to talk to a pastor, priest, or mature Christ-follower about your questions. But if not, or you are ready right now, here is a simple explanation of the gospel of Jesus Christ.

Inside each of us is a God-shaped hole, or an emptiness. We each try to fill this void in our own way. We cannot see on our own that God Himself is the answer to our emptiness. His Spirit has to help us.

The Bible defines sin as attitudes, thoughts, and actions that displease God. Every person since Adam and Eve disobeyed God in the Garden has had this problem. Even if we try really hard to be "good," we still can't reach the standard of holiness of a perfect God.

In Paul's letter to the Roman church, he created a pattern that lays out a path to salvation in Christ. For millions of people, these simple yet profound truths have led to new life. Take your time and read these now. Remember, these are personal to you as God makes His offer of new life.

For ever since the world was created, people have seen the earth and sky. Through everything God made, they can clearly see his invisible qualities—his eternal power and divine nature. So they have no excuse for not knowing God.

Yes, they knew God, but they wouldn't worship him as God or even give him thanks. And they began to think up foolish ideas of what God was like. As a result, their minds became dark and confused. (Romans 1:20–21)

We are made right with God by placing our faith in Jesus Christ. And this is true for everyone who believes, no matter who we are.

For everyone has sinned; we all fall short of God's glorious standard. Yet God, in his grace, freely makes us right in his sight. He did this through Christ Jesus when he freed us from the penalty for our sins. (Romans 3:22–24)

But God showed his great love for us by sending Christ to die for us while we were still sinners. (Romans 5:8)

For the wages of sin is death, but the free gift of God is eternal life through Christ Jesus our Lord. (Romans 6:23)

If you openly declare that Jesus is Lord and believe in your heart that God raised him from the dead, you will be saved. For it is by believing in your heart that you are made right with God, and it is by openly declaring your faith that you are saved. (Romans 10:9–10)

For "Everyone who calls on the name of the LORD will be saved." (Romans 10:13)

For everything comes from him and exists by his power and is intended for his glory. All glory to him forever! Amen. (Romans 11:36)

Countless people have begun a relationship with God through Jesus Christ after reading Paul's words guiding us to salvation. This is the truth of the gospel—the Good News. But God gives you the choice. If you know you are ready to begin a relationship with Him right now, while there are no magic words or no formula for receiving God's gift of salvation, we have included a simple prayer for guidance:

Dear God, I know I am a sinner and need Your forgiveness. I now turn from my sins and ask You into my life to be my Savior and Lord. I choose to follow You, Jesus. Please forgive my sins and give me Your gift of eternal life. Thank You for dying for me, saving me, and changing my life. In Jesus's name, amen.

For I am not ashamed of this Good News about Christ. It is the power of God at work, saving everyone who believes—the Jew first and also the Gentile. (Romans 1:16)

If you prayed the prayer above or have more questions about Jesus, we invite you to call and speak with one of the

K-LOVE pastors. This is a free ministry available for you. They are ready and willing to speak with you right now.

Call 800-525-LOVE (5683)

or

you can scan the QR code below to launch their website.

THANK YOU

To my wife, Casey: I trust Jesus more because of your faithfulness and your love. You are my my favorite.

To my kiddos, Noah, Hannah, and Seth: I know and understand God as a Father from the blessing of being your dad. Thank you for helping me understand joy more than anyone else.

To my parents, Pete and Gay Nell: I learned the devotion and purpose of Jesus from watching your marriage and faith growing up in our home. Thank you for teaching me the firm foundation of faith from the beginning.

To my brother, Daniel: watching your devotion to serve God through these battles the past few years has taught me to hope through any heartaches.

To my cowriter, Robert Noland: as a guy who typically writes songs that last three minutes, I have learned so much from your patience, countenance, and the hard work of serving Jesus on this project. I would not have written this without you and would never want to try.

To Matthew West and AJ Pruis: I have loved the song "Walking Free" since the day we wrote it, and I am so grateful for its inspiration of this book. I'm blown away by the places it has been, and I am honored to have my name next to yours wherever the song goes.

Special thanks to K-LOVE Publishing, Fair Trade Services, Brickhouse Entertainment, all my song cowriters, bandmates, crew, road team, family, and church family.

ABOUT THE AUTHOR

Songwriter and recording artist **MICAH TYLER** writes, performs, and lives out "battle-tested" music that gives glory to his God. Micah is the recipient of multiple Dove and K-LOVE Award nominations, and has written two BMI Top 25 Christian Songs. Along with five number #1 radio hits, his song "Different" is certified Gold by RIAA. Today, Micah's performance schedule ranges from youth camps to conferences to touring with other artists.

Micah's story up until his break-through into commercial success was, in the best sense of the word, *different*. Hailing from the small town of Buna, Texas, he spent his young adult years as a youth pastor. The future artist picked up the guitar to fill the need in his ministry for worship leadership, and from that time God's calling for his life got louder and larger than he could possibly have imagined.

After nine years, Micah left his stable job as youth pastor, moved his family into a single-wide trailer, and began traveling the region performing his music. Micah recalls, "I told the Lord, 'I don't know how to be a professional musician, but you've taught me to be faithful.'" With few connections in the music industry, Micah made ends meet by working as a sausage delivery truck driver while he pursued his calling.

God blessed the steps he and his wife took in faith. Micah's audiences multiplied, and the rest is history. The story of Micah's music career serves as a testimony that, with a little faith and a big God, incredible things are possible.

Based on the hit 2020 song, *Walking Free* is Micah's first book.

Read more about Micah online at www.micahtyler.com.

Writing honest songs that put words to the unspoken is at the heart of every songwriter. Whether it's a melody that uplifts or a lyric that meets people where they are, songwriters chase that connection, the link in the chain of the human experience. When setting out to write songs, Micah Tyler hopes to tell the most authentic stories he can with his own life experiences so he can use his own journey as a ministry to comfort and encourage others. With chart topping hits like "Even Then," "Different," "Amen," & "Walking Free" and more, Micah continues to write and to minister to those around him through music.

Keep in touch with Micah at:
micahtyler.com
and on social media